Caroline Braunmühl
Matter, Affect, AntiNormativity

For Peter

Caroline Braunmühl is a sociologist and an independent scholar. Having earned her first academic degrees at the University of Cape Town and the University of London (Goldsmiths College), she was awarded the degree of Dr. phil. by Universität Hamburg. Her research focuses on poststructuralism as a heterogeneous theoretical movement and, more generally, on social, cultural and political theory, queer theory, and gender studies.

Caroline Braunmühl
Matter, Affect, AntiNormativity
Theory Beyond Dualism

[transcript]

Bibliographic information published by the Deutsche Nationalbibliothek
The Deutsche Nationalbibliothek lists this publication in the Deutsche Nationalbibliografie; detailed bibliographic data are available in the Internet at http://dnb.d-nb.de

© 2022 transcript Verlag, Bielefeld

Cover layout: Maria Arndt, Bielefeld
Translation (chapter 4): Caroline Braunmühl
Printed by Majuskel Medienproduktion GmbH, Wetzlar
Print-ISBN 978-3-8376-6166-8
PDF-ISBN 978-3-8394-6166-2
https://doi.org/10.14361/9783839461662
ISSN of series: 2702-8968
eISSN of series: 2702-8976

Contents

Introduction

"We don't revise a theory, but
construct new ones; we have no
choice but to make others."
*Gilles Deleuze in Deleuze/Foucault
(1980, 208)*

"[T]he claim to escape from the
system of contemporary reality so as
to produce the overall programs of
another society, of another way of
thinking, another culture, another
vision of the world, has led only to
the return of the most dangerous
traditions."
Michel Foucault (1984, 46)

In what ways is poststructuralism implicated in the hegemonic styles
of thinking which it contests or seeks to move beyond? And how can we
shift theory more consequently (or 'radically') beyond such complicity?
These questions form the backdrop to my pursuits in this book.

My specific interest centers on the role of dualism in sustaining
complicity between hegemonic discourses and styles of theorizing
oriented to problematizing, transcending or transgressing these. While
its centrality to hegemonic discourses has been much analyzed –
for instance, in feminist and postcolonial theory – in this book
I aim to show that dualistic thinking also plays a role in recent

counter-hegemonic discourses: Some theorizing associated with the ontological, material and affective turns, queer theory, and current diagnoses of the present tends to exhibit certain dualistic patterns too. This applies even to some of the very theories which specifically purport to leave dualism (or 'the dialectic') behind – such as Michael Hardt's and Antonio Negri's (2001, 140–146, 374–380, 405) or Karen Barad's (2003, 827–829; 2007, 419, n. 27, 429, n.11). That should not surprise us, since it is when we set out to break absolutely with what we oppose that we are most likely unwittingly to engage in a reverse discourse, as alluded by Michel Foucault in the epigraph. As analyzed in much of Cultural Studies, reverse discourse often takes the form of inverting a given dualistic hierarchy into its opposite without, however, questioning its hierarchical arrangement per se. Theorists of colonial discourse and racism, in particular, have contributed much to critiquing forms of oppositional discourse that would, for instance, turn established racialized hierarchies upside down by celebrating the previously devalued category ('the native'; 'black culture'), rather than questioning the underlying hierarchical opposition as such (Hall 1996; Gilroy 1987; 1993; Spivak 1990; Bhabha 1994).

In agreement with this line of problematizing dualism – namely, as hierarchical – I will argue in this book that the critique of dualism is, or should be, an egalitarian project and, conversely, that the reason why it is necessary to move beyond dualistic discourses is that they contribute to legitimizing and sustaining social inequality. This understanding of "dualism" is far from self-evident. It was well-established during the phase of 'high theory' that characterized poststructuralist approaches in Cultural Studies in the Anglophone world in the late twentieth century and continues to inform certain current work that is inflected strongly by deconstruction – such as Judith Butler's or Gayatri Chakravorty Spivak's writings (e.g., Butler 1990; 2015b; Spivak 1990; 2012).

Up until the 1990s it even seemed to form part of critical 'common sense', within poststructuralist theorizing and Cultural Studies, to presuppose that one will be best equipped to minimize complicity with hegemonic discourses when one assumes self-critically that it is impossible to break with them absolutely, once and for all. The term "antagonistic indebtedness" captures this rationale well (Gilroy 1993, 191). It is when we allow for such complicity, and even scrutinize in what ways it might subsist in oppositional discourses, that we can move beyond it to the farthest extent. This book is based upon the rationale that to trace the persistence of dualistic patterns in recent theorizing can assist us in reducing our 'antagonistic indebtedness' to such patterns, and hence, to unegalitarian styles of thinking.

Recent theorizing in the wake of the 'turns' I have mentioned has, however, tended rather to announce itself in terms of a break with what went before, theoretically speaking. As I will seek to show, such rhetoric too is not above producing hierarchical oppositions of its own. As Clare Hemmings (2005), Sara Ahmed (2008) and Carolyn Pedwell (2014) have each pointed out – with reference, respectively, to the ontological turn, to new materialism, and to the distinction between 'paranoid' and 'reparative' styles of critical practice – such self-announcement sometimes comes with a normative hierarchy in which what is offered as theoretically novel is set apart somewhat rigidly from an implicitly unoriginal or old-school 'before'. As glossed by Hemmings, narratives announcing such a break with the theoretical paradigms of an earlier generation at times "tend to the dismissive, and celebrate 'the new' as untouched by whatever we find ourselves currently transcending" (2005, 555). Thus, as Pedwell has shown, 'reparative' and 'paranoid' positions are sometimes juxtaposed as mutually exclusive in a move that – as she seems to imply – marks the first alternative as superior to the second. For instance, when she writes that "critique risks being labelled 'paranoid' and incapable of grappling with the ambivalences of power in the wake of 'the reparative turn'" (2014, 48; see also Pedwell 2014, 58–59, 61–62; Stacey 2014; Barnwell 2016). Arguably, the very term 'paranoid' is sometimes used derogatively – as a distance marker against which to contrast one's own position positively and, hence, as superior (see e.g. Cvetkovich 2012; Love 2007b for examples of this practice). Directly or indirectly, such hierarchizing moves may feed into the maintenance of unegalitarian social arrangements. Perhaps the best example of this is – as I discuss in chapter 3 – the way in which the conventional hierarchy between reason and emotion tends to be inverted, in some work associated with the affective turn, such that 'affect' rather than 'discourse' or 'cognition' has been marked as superior – without, however, questioning either this very hierarchy or the rigid separation of the two categories that enables the normative privilege which either of these terms is assigned. Such either/or-ism[1] permits the categories at hand to remain highly gendered as well as racialized, even if only implicitly: The inversion of the conventional hierarchy between 'reason' and 'emotion' does nothing to upset the discursive order whereby 'reason' remains connoted as masculine and 'white' whereas 'affect' is associated with blackness, along with femininity and the 'queer' (see also Hemmings 2005, 561–562). This applies at least if we understand that axes of social inequality such as gender and race are *implicated* from the start in the classical dualistic oppositions that shape Western-style philosophy and theory, in the sense that these oppositions are constitutively gendered and racialized (Bordo 1986; Benjamin 1988; Flax 1993; Fischer 2016; Bargetz 2015, 583–584). On this understanding of dualism as being linked with unegalitarian social arrangements, only a more complex account of the relationship between 'reason' or 'discourse' and 'emotion' or 'affect' could confound these terms' connotations with (inter alia) masculinity and femininity respectively along with their resonances with gendered, racialized social hierarchies. In order to realize this, we need only to think of the association of blackness as well as femininity with irrationality – and inversely, of irrationality or unreason with femininity as well as blackness – and to take note of the well-established critique of the stereotyped character of any discourse that would seek to find value in this association, thereby affirming rather than subverting it. Such discourse affirms the *intrinsically devaluing* logic of stereotype – which fixes 'the Other' in place (Bhabha 1994, Ch. 3) even when it professes to celebrate the stereotype's content as 'authentic' or a 'positive image'.

Other dualisms which I will analyze in this book, as persisting in recent progressively oriented theorizing, similarly serve to stabilize

---

1   I seem to remember Paul Gilroy using this expression in a course he taught at Goldsmiths College, University of London, in the 1990s.

unegalitarian social orders, as I will detail for the following conceptual pairs – most of them conventional dualisms; one of them a recent (Foucauldian) addition. Each chapter takes up one such pair: successively, I discuss the dualities of matter vs. mind or materiality vs. discourse in Karen Barad's agential realism – a highly prominent variant of new materialism (chapter 1); contrasting variants of the relationship between ontology and epistemology in Barad's work and in Dennis Bruining's, Antonio Negri's and Michael Hardt's (chapter 2); competing recent versions of the discourse/affect hierarchical opposition (chapter 3); the Foucauldian distinction between normalization and normativity, along with its use in recent queer-theoretical writings and diagnoses of the present (chapter 4); and, lastly, the relationship between negativity and affirmation in Sara Ahmed's work on happiness (chapter 5).

Each of these conceptual pairs has recently played a significant part in Cultural Studies – and/or in associated fields for which (post-) poststructuralism forms an important point of reference, such as political theory – in the configuration of a hierarchical opposition. Hierarchies of *matter/mind*, *ontology/epistemology*, *affect/discourse*, *normalization/normativity* and *negativity/affirmation* have all played such a part at the level of what has *structured* recent debate or, more generally, at the level of what structures Cultural Studies and associated disciplines as a discursive field – which is to say that these hierarchical oppositions are not in all cases asserted or addressed as such but, on the contrary, that they are significant for what remains *unquestioned* here; a merely implicit premise. It is a certain – spoken or unspoken – counter-hegemonic consensus that I want to "get at" with my discussion, in the interest of opening up for debate certain taken-for-granted presuppositions which I find problematic.

Preview of chapters

I have tried to arrange the chapters of this book in a way that allows me to pursue a line of inquiry which has oriented me in seeking to flesh out

(1) how thoroughly, in my view, some recent theoretical reflection with a counter-hegemonic orientation has remained implicated in hegemonic logics and orders – namely, in virtue of its dualistic tendencies; (2) just what it is that renders such tendencies problematic – namely, their hierarchizing character and the propensity of much hierarchical thinking to be unegalitarian in thrust (contrary to the intentions of many of its producers), and (3) what kind of discursive style would be most amenable to forestalling our tendency to replicate such effects at the level of theory. In the following preview of the book's individual chapters, I sketch the specific steps by which my line of inquiry proceeds. My problematization of the hierarchical oppositions focused on in each chapter is framed by a metacommentary of sorts, which progresses from one chapter to the next and which I seek to outline in brief below.

1   Matter/Mind

One unspoken premise of a currently highly prominent theoretical approach – that of agential realism (Barad 2003, 2007), a variant of new materialism – pertains to the very understanding of what 'dualism' is and what is problematic about it. This is a significant lacuna in an approach that bases itself in a declared need to leave dualism behind (Barad 2003, 827–829; 2007, 419, n. 27, 429, n.11). But the lacuna does not merely pertain to agential realism, in particular. A need to move beyond 'dualism' has also been accepted on all sides in the debate on new materialism, more generally, which was commenced by Ahmed's (2008) critique of some work central to that overall theoretical movement: the critique that some such work parades as breaking a taboo on studying materiality or 'matter' which it charges (earlier) feminist, 'social constructionist' or poststructuralist theory with having promoted (see chapters 1 and 2 of this book). And yet, despite the consensus stated on all sides of this debate as to the need to transcend dualism, just what accounts for the need to do so was in fact not addressed by most contributors to the debate either.

In chapter 1 I discuss the dualism between matter and mind in the context of further, closely associated dualisms (subject/object; active/passive) with a focus upon agential realism. As will become apparent, Barad – to the extent that she does formulate a critique of dualism at least implicitly – suggests that transcending dualism should mean refusing the very *distinctions* which are at the heart of the conventional dualisms most central to her theoretical approach, such as human/non-human, culture/nature, animate/inanimate but, most central of all, discourse/materiality. As I demonstrate, Barad tends (at times, even if not throughout her work) to designate dualism as problematic, and to be moved beyond, in that it asserts a difference to pertain between the respectively paired terms (see also Gunnarsson 2017, 116, 119–120). I argue that – contrary to this understanding of dualism – distinctions per se are *not* what renders dualistic trends in progressive theorizing complicit with the politics that should be problematized; such as racialized, gendered or even anthropocentric discursive/social orders.

On the contrary: Playing down differences or diluting distinctions is perfectly compatible with maintaining hierarchies (as I demonstrate with a view to Barad's own maintenance of the conventional, highly gendered hierarchy between 'active' and 'passive'). Before indicating why, I want to highlight just how important it is to understand this point when considering recent theoretical trends – even beyond agential realism and new materialism. A small detour through Lena Gunnarsson's recent discussion of the dualism between separateness and inseparability (2017, 117) within debates on intersectionality will help clarify the significance of the insight – which I will develop throughout much of this book with a view to the various dualities to be considered – that *questioning distinctions per se fails to remedy what is politically (and hence also theoretically) most problematic about dualism: This move is not per se any less hierarchizing and, hence, any less implicated in sustaining social inequalities.* While this is not by any means Gunnarsson's own point – she does not attend to the hierarchizing character of dualism at all, but only to its reductiveness – her discussion does underscore the relevance of what I will be critiquing as an assimilationist, identitarian response to dualism within recent theoretical work relating to poststructuralism, especially in Cultural Studies.

Gunnarsson points out that competing sides in debates on intersectionality tend to emphasize *either* separation *or* unity one-sidedly in characterizing the relationship (of interaction/intra-action) between a number of axes of social inequality, such as gender, race and class. Identifying in many different feminist theoretical approaches, more generally (including Barad's), a "tendency [...] to challenge atomistic and dualistic modes of making distinctions by altogether denying separability", she analyzes this as a "mode of reversal" (in resonance with the notion of a reverse discourse upon which I draw) that "in fact reproduces the atomist's basic view of reality: either things are absolutely separate and autonomous, or they cannot be separated at all" (2017, 116; see also Gunnarsson 2013). I would reinterpret the dualism identified by Gunnarsson as "the most basic and problematic of all dualisms, that between separateness and inseparability itself" (Gunnarsson 2017, 117) as a dualism between *difference and sameness* or identity. That the latter forms the underlying, even more fundamental dualism here is suggested by Gunnarsson's own argument, according to which even the mere "tendency [...] to emphasize either *separateness or inseparability* is problematic in itself, since it easily reproduces absolutist and undifferentiated *notions of difference as well as unity*." (2017, 116; emphasis added). "[U]nity" as the dualistic antipode to the term "difference" would seem to amount to 'sameness'; to an absence of *differentiation* altogether rather than merely to 'something less than *separation*'. Difference is hence alternatively hypostatized or negated.

I would rephrase Gunnarsson's analysis, then, to the effect that a *meta-dualism* of sorts between *identity and difference* is at work when it comes to the tendency identified by her within and beyond feminist debates on intersectionality to accentuate either sameness/affinity or difference one-sidedly.[2] Based upon this analysis, it should be easy to

---

2   This analysis already entails in itself — as I will emphasize throughout this book — that the first tendency fails to escape dualistic thinking. Answering dualism

see that hierarchical thinking can be maintained in *either* of these forms. This may be more obvious in the case of classical dualism – i.e. of binary opposition – as theorized in previous work within Cultural Studies and postcolonial theory (see above). That it does apply equally for the tendency, so apparent in Barad's theoretical approach, to understate or water down differences will be demonstrated at length in chapter 1. To anticipate my argument here:

If the difference between the two poles in any one dichotomy is *negated or understated*, one of the poles may yet be privileged as superior, more fundamental, or more important; as the conceptual or (purely) normative standard to which the other term is subordinated, whether explicitly or implicitly. Hierarchies can thus result from *assimilation* (of one term to another) and, hence, a *suppression of differences* between two terms just as readily as they can result from an explicit hierarchical opposition between two terms, of which one is rendered as superior (as occurs in discourses that practice Othering overtly, postulating a superiority of 'male' over 'female' or 'white' over 'black' based upon the assertion of hypostatized differences). Just as much as the first possibility, too, occurs, for instance, in some racialized discourses – namely, in the form of assimilationist universalisms (as analyzed, for instance, by Frantz Fanon [1986] and Roland Barthes [2006a] with a view to French imperialist discourse and rhetoric) – so it applies when differences between such theoretical terms as materiality and discourse, or activity and passivity, are negated or blurred, as I demonstrate in chapter 1 with a view to agential realism. This is why it amounts to a serious misunderstanding to imply, as does Barad, that the problem with dualism is that it *distinguishes* between theoretically fundamental terms as such. I argue in chapter 1 that it is perfectly

---

by privileging similarity or even identity over and against difference is akin to an attempt to break with Hegelian dialectics by a simple act of negation – which, as has been pointed out time and again (Coole 2000; Butler 2012b) (and cannot be repeated often enough), amounts to remaining stuck in 'antithesis', i.e. in the very dialectical logic one seeks to leave behind. To attempt to break with dualism by practicing *the very opposite* of dualism obviously is to remain caught within a dualistic pattern.

possible to distinguish, for instance, subjects from objects in non-hierarchizing terms – that is, in an egalitarian spirit. The critique of dualism should be pursued in such a spirit. If, by contrast, we assume that theoretical distinctions (such as mind/matter) are problematic per se – whether or not they are drawn in a hierarchizing manner – then we will be likely to fail to guard against maintaining just such hierarchizing theoretical models in an *identitarian* form that erases or blurs important differences by way of modeling one term in a given conceptual pair on the other term, which is taken as primary. I will demonstrate in the first chapter of this book that this is what happens in agential realism, in that Barad maintains the conventional masculinist devaluation of passivity vis-à-vis activity in such a form that passivity is literally erased from the universe, while both matter and discourse are construed (and valued) exclusively in terms of their activity. This amounts to inscribing a masculinist dualism – active over passive – at the core of agential realism; as the very basis of its account of mind and matter.

If, as inferable from Gunnarsson's analysis, theoretical discourse tends to shift back and forth between the options of emphasizing difference at the cost of identity or emphasizing identity at the cost of difference, and if, at the same time, we understand dualism as problematic chiefly to the extent that it is hierarchizing, we need to consider identitarian (assimilatory) theoretical models versus theoretical models that hypostatize difference as variants of a meta-dualism that – in *either* variant – arranges conceptual counterparts in hierarchical terms, privileging the one term over the other by rendering it as primary or superior. Whether this occurs by way of opposing two terms to one another as mutually exclusive, or in the form of conflating them: in either case, what is in need of critique is the hierarchical opposition at hand. Theory is *not* complicit with hegemonic order in virtue of drawing distinctions – even fundamental distinctions such as the ones between discourse and materiality, active and passive or subjects and objects. Theory *operates* by drawing distinctions; it could not possibly proceed otherwise. It is only when a given distinction – or, alternatively, an identitarian assimilation of terms – entails any kind of *hierarchical opposition* between the terms in question, whether explicitly or implicitly, that either move may become complicit with hegemonic orders, namely, when such oppositions stabilize *social inequalities*. Chapter 1 sets out in further detail, and concretizes based on the example of agential realism, why dualism should *really* be considered problematic: namely, due to it its participation in hierarchical thinking. *This* is what risks rendering theory complicit with social inequality, even when it is intended critically.

2   Ontology/Epistemology

The recent 'turns' in critical theorizing seem to emphasize difference at the cost of similarity or continuity whenever they normatively privilege 'the opposite' of those lines of theorizing from which they declare themselves to depart: It is obvious that the 'ontological turn' signals a turn *away* from epistemology, at least as a (similarly) one-sided pursuit. The same can be said of the affective turn in its self-positioning vis-à-vis an earlier discursive or cognitive emphasis. 'Negativity' and 'affirmation', too, tend to be played against each other (e.g. Halberstam 2011; Braidotti 2002), partially in the guise of a 'reparative' turn (Cvetkovich 2012; critically: Barnwell 2016; Pedwell 2014; Stacey 2014). It should be clear from the above that it is not my project to seek to answer this tendency to highlight distinctness, if not opposition, with a contrary tendency to privilege continuity or similarity instead. It is, as Gunnarsson has shown so convincingly, the very dichotomization of these alternatives that is problematic. The alternatives of privileging *either* 'sameness' *or* 'difference' narrow down thinking to two options as if these exhausted the spectrum of theoretical possibilities. The critique of dualism seeks to make *further alternatives* thinkable again. It is in search of such alternatives that, from chapter 2 onwards, I explore a third overall possibility for thinking difference, beyond the identitarian versus dichotomizing discursive logics addressed above.

This is the possibility of theorizing difference as relationality-in-tension. I set out what this might mean, and the effects of doing so, in chapter 2 in the context of discussing the relationship between epistemology and ontology. I consider this third possibility as a theoretically and politically rewarding alternative to the recently prominent and widespread dilution of difference (e.g. between matter and mind) which goes hand in hand with the mistaken criticism of distinctions as in themselves dualistic, addressed in chapter 1. My critical discussion of this tendency is simultaneously continued into chapter 2. Here I clarify with a focus upon the ontological turn that to *either* dichotomize ontological and epistemological pursuits against each other (as has occurred in Hardt's and Negri's work) *or* seek to reconcile them as part of a single *"ethico-onto-epistem-ology"* as if such fusion entailed no loss (as does Barad [2007, 185; emphasis in the original]) can go hand in hand with producing a hierarchical opposition whereby ontology is privileged, explicitly or implicitly, over and against epistemology. Such a bias generates necessary blind spots in one's analysis of power relations when it comes to the politics of knowledge, including the discursive, perspectival and therefore partial status of one's own theorizing. At the same time, to invert this hierarchy, such that epistemology is privileged over and against ontology, will merely produce necessary analytico-political blind spots of another kind, to the detriment of materialist analyses of power. I demonstrate this latter point through a critical discussion of Dennis Bruining's recent intervention (2016) into the debate on new materialism mentioned above. Bruining conceptually subordinates materiality to discourse and, by extension, ontology to epistemology in a hierarchizing fashion that is a mere mirror image of Barad's attempt to fuse the two at the price of tacitly subordinating epistemology.

As an alternative to any such hierarchical opposition between epistemology and ontology, I turn to some early work by Spivak which is oriented by deconstruction (see also Pedwell 2014). Deconstruction as practiced by her – namely, as a means of social critique; a critique of unequal power relations – emphasizes tension as a form of relationality. This provides a fruitful means of avoiding the twin traps of hypostatizing or collapsing difference, both of which tend to maintain hierarchical thinking. In chapter 2 I exemplify the productivity of this approach by arguing that the epistemological and ontological perspectives form each others' constitutive outsides, such that only when one holds them together without privileging either perspective as a matter of principle, whilst at the same time acknowledging their incommensurability (i.e. the tension between them), can we do justice to how *each* of these perspectives renders apparent certain aspects of power whilst making others imperceptible – thereby generating effects of power of its own (as any discourse does). In this way, my discussion of the relationship between ontology and epistemology exemplifies how we can circumvent the twin problems of diluting distinctions or rendering them as mutually exclusive oppositions in favor of doing justice to *both difference and relationality*. The latter alternative is more readily amenable to an egalitarian perspective, understood as an orientation critical of all forms of social inequality.

3   Affect/Discourse

In reflecting, next, on how discourse and affect may be related to one another theoretically, I concretize one specific conceptual possibility for thinking relationality as tension, as a potential route towards the goal of drawing distinctions without establishing conceptual/normative hierarchies that resonate with unegalitarian social arrangements. In chapter 3, I explore the rhetorical figure of the chiasm – a crossing – as invoked fleetingly in some of Butler's recent work, as a concept-metaphor which, in some sense, extends the model of intersectionality (developed initially with a view to the relationship between race and gender) (Crenshaw 1991) to apply to the theorization of difference, more generally.

Much research on affect, emotion and feeling is characterized either by an identitarian reduction of affect to its discursive dimension or, alternatively, by a binary opposition between affect and discourse. In both cases, a hierarchy is usually maintained, which either subordinates affect to the discursive or privileges it over the discursive. This is to reproduce the conventional hierarchy between reason (or discourse) and emotion – whether straightforwardly or in inverted form, that is, by celebrating 'affect' whilst maligning 'discourse'. Yet in order to overcome this hierarchy, it is not enough merely to invert it, for that would amount to a mere reverse discourse, as pointed out earlier. I argue that *either* variant of thinking the relationship between affect/emotion and discourse hierarchically is complicit with unegalitarian (gendered, racialized) discourses that are implicated in sustaining social inequality.

Based upon the model of the chiasm, I explore an alternative to the above modes of thinking about discourse and affect, which would be less prone to such complicity. I propose to conceive of feeling and discourse as *mutually implicating, yet irreducible to one another*. This would enable us to envisage discourse and affect as potentially impacting each other in either direction, whether in the form of mutual congruence or of dynamic tension – contrary to any model that would posit one of these terms as ultimately primary in accounting for the other. I clarify the theoretical-political import of the proposed model for theorizing the relationship between emotion and discourse by way of contrast with Margaret Wetherell's concept of affective-discursive practice (2012; 2015), which – as I argue – subordinates affect to discourse in an assimilatory, ultimately identitarian fashion by way of reducing it to a discursive/performative practice. By reference to "double-edged thinking" as practiced by Butler (2004b, 129), I detail how the model I develop can do justice to the saturation of both discourse and affect with (bio-) power, providing us with a critical, politicized notion of these terms. This is fruitful, as I conclude, for an egalitarian, feminist, intersectional theory as much as for a practical politics of emotion.

4   Normalization/Normativity

To think difference without either hypostatizing or downplaying it could mean thinking relationality in terms of *connection and tension at once*, then, rather than accentuating connection one-sidedly – to the detriment of differentiation or even contrast. The latter alternative would ultimately amount to *suppressing conflict*, whether in the form of (logical) contradiction or (social) antagonism. The risk of suppressing conflict should move us to appreciate the fact that distinctions (or, put in other words, *categories*) as such are emphatically not 'the enemy'.

We must not be phobic, and have no reason to be phobic or averse, to identifying differences between fundamental theoretical terms which form counterparts to each other. On the contrary: *collapsing difference* (such as when 'discourse' becomes indistinguishable from 'materiality', as tends to occur in agential realism [chapters 1 and 2]) *is antithetical to relational thinking*. For, to speak of a 'relationship' in any meaningful way in fact presupposes that the terms being related to one another are *mutually distinct*, much as they may be mutually connected *at the same time* (see also Gunnarsson 2013, 14). What we should problematize is not, then, the distinctness of terms, that is, the assertion of differences between, for instance, 'materiality' and 'discourse' or 'discourse' and 'affect'. What matters instead for a counter-hegemonic theoretical politics is precisely *how* we construe such terms to differ from – and to relate to – one another.

The notion of a chiasm or crossing, a crosscurrent, in terms of which I construe the difference/relationship between 'affect' and 'discourse' in chapter 3, has appeal in that it enables us to envisage theoretical terms as at once distinct and mutually implicated – in other words, as neither entirely separable nor therefore 'the same'. It enables us to allow room, in critical theorizing, for contradistinction, discrepancy, and conflict without sacrificing relational thinking (a fundamental of feminist, antiracist and other theories critiquing unequal power *relations*). The notion of a chiasm is, however, only one amongst a number of concepts that hold promise for a pursuit of the line of theorizing which I seek to promote as best suited to moving beyond dualism, understood as complicit with social relations of domination – namely, a line of theorizing that, while it is not necessarily *identified* with deconstruction, is certainly inflected by it, and of which I see Butler and Spivak as the most able practitioners. Such theorizing is profoundly relational in a manner that highlights, and respects, distinction as much as connection in the manner in which relationality is approached: in terms of tension, ambiguity (or the "double-edged" [Butler, see above]), and even conflict.

Theorizing that is critical of inequality must in fact be maximally attentive to conflict if it is to steer clear as much as possible of obscuring unequal relations of power. Put the other way round: Counteracting complicities of our own theorizing with relations of domination requires us to render power relations maximally apparent. And this task is advanced by an attention to conflict: namely, to the extent that inequality breeds conflict, if it *is* not actually a form of conflict. To suppress or obscure conflict effectively is to risk furthering social inequality (if "only" by obscuring it in turn).

A further concept, which is more prominent in Butler's work than the figure of the chiasm, is particularly suited to analyzing relations of power and inequality; in that (amongst the possible forms of conflict or tension) it brings processes of *exclusion* to the fore. This is the concept of a constitutive outside. While it will figure in my analyses of other dualities in the earlier chapters, in chapter 4 this concept takes center stage. Here I deepen my earlier discussion of (bio-) power in chapter 3, where this term comes into play in relation to discourse as well as affect. In chapter 4, I consider Foucault's work along with certain diagnoses of the present which follow in its steps, within and beyond queer theory, as developed in German. Just as the figure of a chiasm is productive for thinking difference relationally and, at the same time, in terms of tensions, so the notion of a constitutive outside enables us – specifically with a view to power – to think exclusion and inclusion, 'outside' and 'inside', 'positive' and 'negative' dimensions of power as interconnected, rather than rendering one of these dimensions invisible while focusing upon the other one, thereby dissociating the two. This forms my project in chapter 4.

The central conceptual dyad which I will consider here consists in the distinction, drawn by Foucault at one point in his work, between *normativity* and *normalization*. In this case, I thus complement my focus, in all other chapters, upon conceptual pairs that form the stuff of classical dualism through a rather recent addition to the list. What motivates my choice of the particular conceptual counterparts I focus upon in this book is, in each case, the significant role they play within recent work in Cultural Studies and its vicinity. Since, however, a use of the term 'normalization' in contradistinction from the term 'normativity' – as developed in Foucault's later work and within the pertinent German-language literature – is less common in the Anglophone world, at least within queer theory, below I spend some time introducing my discussion in chapter 4.

It is virtually commonplace to state that Foucault, and many of those drawing upon his work, criticize a juridical, negative conception of power and analyze power in ways more attuned to its productivity. This project can, however, be exaggerated in such a way that power's productive side is emphasized one-sidedly, to the detriment of its exclusionary and constraining effects. The tenor of my argument in chapter 4 is that to focus one-sidedly upon power's 'positive' and 'flexible' modes of operation is – considered from an intersectional perspective – to risk emphasizing the ways in which it operates for the more privileged amongst us while 'forgetting' its effects for those at the social margins. By contrast, to analyze power in terms of the concept of a constitutive outside is to do so in strictly relational terms. It is to consider social exclusion *constitutive* of the manner in which power may well operate for many subjects in the present, as has been widely argued (if with implicit reference to the global North only): by way of *in*cluding them within a normality which for the last several decades has been shaped by the neoliberal injunction for subjects 'positively' to construct themselves in line with the notions of optimization and self-responsibility. For subjects positioned at least ambiguously with a view to gender, race, sexuality and/or in that – for instance – they undergo psychiatric treatment, are unemployed long-term, or confined in a refugee camp, 'neoliberalism' can mean finding oneself addressed, not merely (if at all) by the said injunction, but (at least simultaneously) by a biopolitical interpellation that would question whether you are a subject who is actually *capable* of living up to that injunction. If we do not see this but instead focus only on power's effects for the more privileged – and if (in the worst case) we theorize power as such based only on how it makes itself known, and felt, to these – then we risk *reinforcing* the inequality of power's differential operation for differently situated subjects. We risk reinforcing, as I argue in chapter 4, subalternity by obscuring the negativity or rigidity of power at the level of our analysis and theorization of the social. I see this risk as given in the context of some recent diagnoses of the present. It can be traced back to Foucault's own work, upon which they draw. This is why I spend a good part of the chapter with a close reading of his *Security, Territory, Population* and *The Birth of Biopolitics* – those of Foucault's lecture series at the Collège de France which instantiate this risk most clearly (Foucault 2007; 2010).

The distinction between the terms 'normativity' and 'normalization' is closely related to the better-known distinction between discipline and governmentality. Whereas in *Discipline and Punish* (Foucault 1991), Foucault tended to use the terms 'normalizing' and 'normative' interchangeably, in *Security, Territory, Population* he proposed a fundamental distinction between 'normalization' and 'normativity' (though only at one specific point [Foucault 2007, 55–63], of which much has been made in some publications in German, however). While in Foucault's earlier, synonymous usage of the terms 'normative' and 'normalizing', *both* these terms were closely associated with disciplinary power and, as such, with a deployment of norms, 'normalization' in Foucault's later usage is characterized – in contrast with 'normativity' (a juridical technology of power) as well as 'normation' (a disciplinary technology of power) – as *operating essentially in a manner other than through norms*. As such, Foucault now redefined normalization as operating along the lines of apparatuses of security (*dispositifs*), governmentality and neoliberalism.

Normalization in this new sense may involve norms, too, but these are developed on the basis of statistical *description*. Rather than being defined from the very first by norms that operate *prescriptively*, the normal here is to be understood, in the first place, as a matter of demographic distribution; as *statistical* normality, rather than as a matter of evaluation, or devaluation, in terms of norms (Foucault 2007, 56–63; see also Amir/Kotef 2018). As such normalization is flexible and inclusive rather than binary as well as exclusionary (cf. Foucault 2007, 6, 46–49, 56–63; see also Foucault 2010, 259–260), as in the opposition normal/abnormal which underpins normation.

My close reading of Foucault in chapter 4 critiques the Foucauldian narrative – within and beyond his own work – whereby neoliberalism operates largely without relying on norms or prescription. It critiques

Foucault's implicit representation of statistical techniques (the basis of governmentality, as defined by apparatuses of security [*dispositifs*]) as descriptive in the sense that they are free of normative evaluation and devaluation. Contrary to this narrative, I argue that even a statistical notion of 'the normal' as an average or a range of numerical distribution is not devoid of evaluation and (therefore) implicit prescription. Drawing upon Butler's account of how norms operate, I point out that a hierarchical distinction from the 'abnormal' is constitutive of *any possible notion* of the 'normal', however much such notions may parade as 'merely empirical'. Foucault's implicit juxtaposition of evaluation to description, which (as I demonstrate in chapter 4) underpins the difference he outlines between disciplinary power and neoliberalism, between normation and normalization has the consequence of obfuscating *unequal* relations of power. In fact he explicitly disputed that neoliberalism relies upon social exclusion (Foucault 2010, 259; see also Foucault 2010, 227–229 and – for further detail – chapter 4 below). This is what renders his account of neoliberalism unproductive and deeply problematic from an intersectional perspective – unless it is supplemented by a more critical, expanded understanding of normativity.

I argue that such an understanding is offered by Butler. Contrary to readings of Butler that construe her account of norms, and of power more generally, as predominantly negative, (gendered) norms according to her operate *at once* productively and restrictively. Thus 'sex' is to be understood *as* a norm "which *qualifies a body for life* within the domain of cultural intelligibility" *on the basis of* abjecting other bodies as unintelligible (Butler 1993, 2; emphasis added). Drawing on this more integrated view of norms as cutting both ways – as constituting subjects based upon processes of abjection, i.e. upon constitutive exclusion – I propose to conceive of normativity much more widely than did Foucault: not as a specifically juridical, negative modality of power to be *opposed* to positive modalities of power (see above) but as the dimension of evaluation (i.e. the value-laden and implicitly prescriptive dimension) which frames any possible discourse, and any technology of power, inescapably. Further, I propose to conceive of neoliberalism as deploying techniques of normalization and normation *in tandem* and as *each equally normative*. Neoliberal normalization as a technology of power describes the ways power is encountered and undergone predominantly by those who manage to pass for (more or less) 'normal'. Normalization is normative in that it is the devaluing notion of the 'abnormal', the specter of being ('found' to be) abnormal, that incites subjects to seek to pass for normal, in the first place – even as not everyone succeeds in doing so. Normation is hence the other side of the coin; both technologies of power must be viewed as being *constitutively interrelated* from an intersectional point of view, and as a form of biopolitics: 'Normation' refers to how those less successful in this collective movement of differentiation from the 'abnormal' – those 'found' to *embody* the abnormal – undergo and encounter power, even if they simultaneously find themselves exposed to the *normalizing* injunction to optimize themselves. 'Normation' thus refers to the processes of exclusion (abjection) which form normalization's constitutive outside; its enabling frame. Normalization must not, then, be juxtaposed to normation, nor to normativity, as if qua specifically *neoliberal* technology of power it could exist independently of either normation qua *disciplinary* technology of power, or as if it were essentially post-normative.

As chapter 4 concludes, based upon the analysis sketched above, it is untenable to picture neoliberal normalization as a flexible rather than binary, and an inclusive rather than exclusionary *alternative* to disciplinary (or juridical) modalities of power. For, normalization operates in conjunction with normation on the basis of an ultimately binary normative matrix which continues to juxtapose 'normal' to 'abnormal' (see also Amir/Kotef 2018, 249). My proposal for reframing the relationship between, and hence the meaning of, the terms 'normativity', 'normation' and 'normalization' remedies the false opposition between statistical, i.e. empirical description and normative prescription established by Foucault in his later work. This opposition is implicitly at work wherever neoliberal normalization is situated outside normation and/or normativity – as a separate, free-standing technology of power which forms their post-normative other. Much as in Foucault's own later work, in the German-language literature referring to Foucault this occurs in a form such that normalization qua neoliberal technology of power is said to have tended to replace, or to render politically less significant, modalities of power that would operate in exclusionary ways based upon stigmatizing, binary norms which divide the 'normal' from the 'abnormal'. In this context normalization has been opposed to normativity in the sense of two mutually independent technologies of power while Foucault's third term, normation, has been virtually ignored (Ludwig 2016b; Bargetz/ Ludwig 2015; Engel 2002) – hence the title of chapter 4. Such diagnoses are to an extent euphemistic, since in accentuating only or primarily the inclusive and productive face of how power operates in the present, they obscure its exclusionary and repressive face.

In the Anglophone world, a few recent interventions into queer theory have involved a comparable move when it comes to accentuating positive-productive dimensions of power conceptually, whilst dissociating these from power's negative (exclusionary) dimensions in my assessment: Annamarie Jagose, Robyn Wiegman and Elizabeth A. Wilson have charged that to read *norms* as operating primarily negatively, in a restrictive and exclusionary manner, as has occurred in much of queer theory according to them, is to reinstate a version of the 'repressive hypothesis' as problematized by Foucault (Foucault 1990; Jagose 2015; Wiegman/Wilson 2015). In my view, these writers risk using this charge as a springboard for leaping in the very opposite direction, of privileging norms' inclusionary and generative effects – thereby dissociating the productive and the repressive sides of norms, and of power, from each other in what remains a somewhat dualistic pattern, rather than working towards their mutual theoretical integration. I agree, however, with the view that much queer theory has advanced a primarily negative construction of norms as *policing*, *stigmatizing*, and *pathologizing* those disqualified as 'abnormal' sexually or in gendered terms. In fact, within English-language queer theory, the terms 'normativity' and 'normalization' (or 'normative'/'normalizing') have been used at least by some more approximately as synonyms or closely associated terms, whose difference from one another seems hard to pin down, than as oppositions (Berlant/Warner 1998, 552–553, 557; Hall/Jagose 2013, xvi; Wiegman/Wilson 2015, 7, 10, 18). Such use of these terms to indicate a predominantly negative conception of norms pertaining especially to sexuality and gender contrasts with the opposition between the same terms which has been constructed in German-language publications, as briefly sketched above. At the same time it contrasts with Foucault's own conception of disciplinary power as "at-once prohibitive *and productive*" (Jagose 2015, 39; emphasis added) – from which Foucault would distinguish a more exclusively productive version of power slightly later, in his lectures on governmentality and neoliberalism (Foucault 2007; 2010; see above). (Jagose, Wiegman and Wilson do not reference Foucault's work on neoliberalism and governmentality but cite solely *The History of Sexuality*, Volume 1 [1990].) It is the potential of Foucault's earlier analysis of disciplinary power for developing a *double-edged* notion of power as well as norms – as it comes to fuller fruition in Butler's work – that chapter 4 highlights, contrary to readings of Foucault and/or Butler that would compartmentalize their respective theoretical contributions in terms of a dichotomy between productive vs. negative views of power (Jagose 2015). (While Butler's account of norms may be at risk of being read as predominantly negative due to its emphasis upon exclusion, this would thwart its potential of doing justice to, and of mutually articulating, both sides of power – productive and harmful, even annihilating – as *interdependent*.)

In the (queer-theoretical) reception of Foucault (and Butler) in different languages, then, the terms 'normativity' and 'normalization', or 'normative' and 'normalizing', have been construed alternatively as mutually exclusive *or* as close to synonymous. (Each of these uses of the two terms can be read as drawing upon different phases in Foucault's work, respectively: his analyses of disciplinary power versus governmentality.) This phenomenon resonates with the one identified by Gunnarsson regarding debates on intersectionality (see above), in that a meta-dualism seems to be at work in virtue of which different writers highlight *either* 'identity' *or* 'difference' in their use of the conceptual pair 'normalization/normativity' – with the effect, in this case, that *positive-formative and negative-exclusionary dimensions of power are dichotomized against one another.* In post-Foucauldian (as well as Foucault's own later) theorizing too, then, we encounter a certain dualistic 'either/or-ism'. It is this overall tendency towards splitting – which takes different forms in Germany/Austria than it does in the Anglophone context – that I ultimately wish to critique in chapter 4. On both sides of this conceptual divide, however, Foucault's work is idealized and shielded from critique, as I argue – a somewhat one-sided approach to what I assess as an ambiguous tone on his part when it comes to neoliberalism's political 'innovations'.

To analyze power either as primarily 'productive' *or* 'negative', 'flexible' *or* 'rigid' (a terminology more common in German-language settings) is mutually to dissociate its *differential* operation for differentiated categories of subjects. This amounts to an unrelational perspective, and one which obviously privileges either dimension of power at the cost of the other. Either of the above one-sided versions of 'power', whether predominantly 'negativist' or 'productivist', amount to producing (yet again) a hierarchical opposition, if only implicitly: in conceptual rather than purely normative terms. They do so in the sense of producing an epistemic bias which renders invisible the fact that *power is encountered and undergone differently depending* in part *upon subjects' social positionality.* My own proposal for a theorization of the relationship between the terms 'normalization', 'normation' and 'normativity' (previewed above) – drawing as it does upon Butler's account of norms – offers an alternative to the polarized construction of norms, and of power, as *either* primarily positive *or* primarily negative; contrary to any reading of Butler that would see her as privileging a negative notion of norms as well as power in line with the 'repressive hypothesis' (Jagose 2015). On my reading, the concept of a constitutive outside as employed by Butler works against such polarization through its rigorously relational emphasis, which forces us to consider the negativities that circumscribe power's productive effects without understating the latter. Theorizing exclusion as constitutive of all social inclusion is to conceive of 'outside' and 'inside', not as separate (as in a binary opposition), but as inseparably intertwined, yet distinct and even contrary in its effects for differently positioned categories of subjects.

In contrast, situating neoliberal normalization outside normativity by dissociating it from disciplinary normation (as occurs in the German-language diagnoses of the present discussed in chapter 4) is to dissociate the social inclusion of the more privileged from the exclusion/abjection of everyone else. This amounts to obscuring, and therefore in a sense to reproducing, the violence of social exclusion. At the same time, the alternative of diluting all difference between normalization and normativity, while connoting both terms negatively, i.e. with power's negative dimensions (as has occurred in English-language queer theory), not only risks overlooking how power – and normativity – is implicated in even the most seemingly 'autonomous' or 'transgressive' practices (as Wiegman and Wilson point out [2015]) (see also below). Which would be, likewise, to understate the extent to which power saturates social relations. It is also specifically to understate the *inequality* of power's differential operation for different subjects. What allows us to move beyond either of these alternatives, and their respective complicity with unegalitarian social arrangements, is to posit a *tension* between the 'positive' and 'negative' faces of power whilst recognizing their interconnection. This will contribute to rendering social inequality and its violence maximally apparent.

5   Negativity/Affirmation

In my introduction to this book so far, I have problematized hierarchical thinking as potentially complicit with unegalitarian social orders. But the reflections pursued in chapters 1 through 4 beg a question which is politically decisive: If, as I argue, both classically dualistic thinking and its identitarian counterpart can be complicit with inequality to the extent that they are hierarchizing, does this mean that *any* conceptual/normative hierarchy is per se unegalitarian? The earlier chapters in this book leave open this question. This is acceptable because they each focus upon a specific hierarchical opposition in progressive theorizing which *does* contribute to sustaining social inequality. In the book's final chapter, chapter 5, however, the above question is addressed head-on.

Doing so is all the more important given my position, developed in chapter 4, that all discourse is inherently normative (see above). In other words, a *non*-normative discourse is impossible. But where does this leave critical and progressively oriented theorizing? Is all theorizing necessarily complicit with social inequality? These are the larger questions which form the backdrop to chapter 5. If the latter question is answered in the negative – as it must be if there is to be any notion of a counter-hegemonic discourse – then we need to ask how we can distinguish hegemonic forms of *normativity* from counter-hegemonic ones: If it is possible to envisage a counter-hegemonic kind of normativity, then what qualifies it as counter-hegemonic? Would such a form of normativity be non-hierarchizing? Or how else can we conceive of an egalitarian, critical normativity?

I take the view that normativity (i.e. all discourse) is intrinsically hierarchizing, but not therefore necessarily unegalitarian. Normativity is per se hierarchizing only *in a certain sense*: in the sense that the evaluative dimension of any discourse entails a *value* hierarchy; a distinction between better and worse, important and less important. (Whether it be as a matter of overt evaluation or of what value judgments are implicit in the kinds of conceptual prioritization, the epistemic – and hence, perceptual – biases entailed in a given conceptual architecture, as argued with a view to some of the hierarchical oppositions considered in this book.) It is necessary to distinguish, then, between the hierarchizing character of normativity as such, on the one hand, and thought that is hierarchizing in the sense that it is unegalitarian, on the other (in its ultimate trajectory if not in intention). This raises the further question: What could a counter-hegemonic form of (normative/conceptual) hierarchization possibly look like?

The above questions and my answers to them are threaded through this book's final chapter, but are not treated in the abstract. Rather, I negotiate them in the context of yet another conceptual dyad: negativity vs. affirmation. This dyad is not approached directly, however, but via the relationship between unhappiness and happiness; affects that are closely related to these respective orientations. If in chapter 4, normativity is considered critically, in terms of how a hegemonic normativity sustains inequality, in chapter 5 normativity comes into play in a more affirmative sense: Here I am in search of a *normative style* that would encompass both negativity and affirmation, and that would relate both to one another in a non-dualistic fashion. We will find that how we orient to happiness and to unhappiness, respectively (negatively and/or affirmatively) – and how we frame these feelings' relationship to one another (dualistically or as potentially contiguous, yet in tension) – is important to this search.

Specifically, chapter 5 concludes this book with what I intend to be a tribute to Ahmed's work on happiness (2007; 2010). I can critique her work as sternly, as engagedly as I do only because it has guided my thinking on this subject so decisively; because in my estimation it comes so close to 'getting it right'. It is, in other words, in good part from Ahmed's own insights that I draw the means of critiquing Ahmed at those points where I find certain ambiguities in her work to reach the point of contradiction – a contradiction from which I feel that there is still more to learn. And it is from the example provided by Ahmed's treatment of happiness and unhappiness that I glean the criteria by which I propose to distinguish a *counter-hegemonic normative style* from a hegemonic one.

The chapter offers a close reading of Ahmed's work on happiness, with *The Promise of Happiness* (Ahmed 2010) placed center stage. I identify a tension, even a contradiction between her critique of *hegemonic* framings of 'happiness' and her tendency to reject happiness *as such*, however understood: Ahmed's critique of hegemonic framings of happiness – to the effect that these result in social exclusion and a devaluation of the unhappy – is unintelligible in its critical force except when happiness per se is avowed as desirable. Otherwise, there could be nothing objectionable about the unequal social distribution of un-/happiness, as critiqued by her. Whereas Ahmed's rejection of happiness amounts to a reverse discourse in my assessment, there are other moments in her theorizing in which she offers an affirmative, alternative framing of the term. It is in a non-dualistic framing of happiness and unhappiness, which refuses to dismiss *either* of these emotions, that her account is most consequently egalitarian (that is, critical of social exclusion).

I maintain, furthermore, that the competing strands of Ahmed's argument exemplify differing normative styles – one mimicking a hegemonic normativity, the other instantiating an alternative, queer normativity. I contest the notion of queer "antinormativity", which styles queer theory as normatively innocent (Wiegman/Wilson 2015): Far from being value-neutral or non-hierarchizing, queer theory too participates in promoting normative priorities. At its best, however, a queer normative style is *non-normalizing*. Instead of reifying value hierarchies, it denaturalizes attributions of value in an egalitarian spirit. It is most in line with this spirit when Ahmed, at some points in her writing, reclaims happiness by offering an alternative, counter-hegemonic framing of what it might mean to be affected positively. Happiness as such cannot be rejected wholeheartedly, I insist. For, it is implicitly being affirmed as desirable in any impulse to escape suffering, in all political struggle, and in the very hope for change.

In this book's final chapter, then, I seek to advance an orientation (theoretical as much as practical) that avows ambiguity (see also Pedwell 2014; Stacey 2014): I emphasize the political potential of allowing for contiguity between happiness and unhappiness without conceptually collapsing the tension between these emotions into a pseudo-harmony that would suppress conflict between them. (Here I take my cue from Ahmed's exemplary challenge: her call on us to open up to, even to *bear*, unhappiness' interference with happiness.) Contrary to Ahmed as I read her, however, I ask that neither of these emotions be hierarchized over and against the other in a fashion that would suppress ambiguity by splitting it into an affirmation of the one state vs. a rejection of the other: If affirming happiness must not be allowed to tilt over into a negation of unhappiness, neither must we give preference to unhappiness (as if that were at all possible). For either move would be *unegalitarian* in effect, as I argue in chapter 5. Instead, I make the case for orienting to each of these emotions in a way that entails moments of negativity *as well as* affirmation. This chapter foregrounds contiguity and simultaneity, then, not in the sense of pure continuity, of a fusion that would blur boundaries to the point of negating them, but (once again) in terms of a double-edged and even tense or conflicted relationship.

For, as I argue throughout this book, when it comes to dualism and the assimilatory, ultimately identitarian response to it which I critique, it is by allowing for ambiguity and tension that we are better equipped for reducing theory's complicities with hegemonic, unegalitarian orders. We need to find alternatives to the meta-dualism of privileging *either* difference *or* affinity (Gunnarsson; see above) *because both of these alternatives tend to further unegalitarian tendencies.* Qua corollary of the kind of deconstructively inclined social thought which I view as best suited to moving beyond such tendencies, affirming ambiguity and tension as a way of affirming relationality requires us also to take contradictions – such as the contradiction which I trace in Ahmed's work on happiness – seriously rather than dismissing or diluting their significance. We thus need to recognize contradictions as problems, as a reason for transforming (theory) further (Butler 2012b; Coole 2000). Only if we do so can we truly take others seriously – and even ourselves; our own writing.

With chapters 4 and 5, I broach the subject of normativity and antinormativity announced in the title of this book, as its third central subject alongside 'matter' and 'affect'. In concluding this volume, I contest a certain, often unspoken premise of queer theory to the effect that if hegemonic normativity is politically problematic, our response should be to abstain from normativity as such – as if that were at all possible. In my view, this amounts to a misunderstanding of self; a misunderstanding of one's own interventions as *non*-normative, which only serves to cover up the 'will to power'; the inextricable connection between knowledge and power (as asserted by Foucault [1980]).[3] As such

---

3   Foucault's insistence that there is no knowledge outside power is contradicted in my assessment by the uncritical opposition between statistical vs. normative

it is a politically consequential fallacy: It produces *unacknowledged* effects of power.

It is such (often) tacit premises of theoretical discourse – the notion that it is possible to rid one's own discourse of normativity; the understanding of dualism as an assertion of differences best transcended by contesting boundaries as such – that I seek to question and thus to open up for collective reflection, in the hope that this will contribute to advancing critical discourses in Cultural Studies and (post-) poststructuralism by way of clarifying – and, where necessary, changing – their conceptual, normative, and political thrust.

I seek to intervene, then, in what remains *un*debated and unquestioned in these fields, or is at least not debated enough: in what remains (too) taken for granted. I do so with the goal of contributing to rendering theory in these fields not only more consequently self-reflexive, but also more consequently (or 'radically') egalitarian. It is in what remains unthought, in what we could refer to as theory's 'unconscious' that we are most likely to remain complicit with hegemonic discourses precisely because this happens inadvertently.

knowledge which underwrites his juxtaposition of governmentality vs. disciplinary power (see above and chapter 4).

1 Matter/Mind
The Persistence of Hierarchical Opposition in Karen Barad's Agential Realism
Or: Why Move Beyond Dualism?

Introduction

In recent years a debate has developed regarding the question of whether new materialism really does move beyond fundamental dualisms such as that between culture and materiality, as its proponents purport (according to the contributors to this debate, namely Ahmed 2008; Bruining 2013; Davis 2009; Hinton/Liu 2015; Irni 2013; Sullivan 2012; van der Tuin 2008; Willey 2016; see also Coleman 2014; Davis 2014; Jagger 2015). Thus Sara Ahmed has argued that some writers associated with new materialism, such as Elizabeth Grosz, Elizabeth Wilson and Karen Barad, risk reproducing this dualism when they portray earlier feminist or poststructuralist work as having privileged culture one-sidedly to the detriment of an adequate account of materiality, which only new materialism is supposedly equipped to provide (Ahmed 2008; see also Bruining 2013; Hemmings 2011, 101; McNeil 2011, 436). Yet exactly what it is about such dualisms that makes it necessary to move beyond them from a feminist perspective is not spelled out by the contributors to this debate, with the exception of Peta Hinton (2013; see below). Accordingly, it is less than clear what theoretical strategies are most suited to accomplishing this goal.

Lena Gunnarsson (2013), while not a direct contributor to the debate on new materialism, has recently raised the question of what it means to transcend dualism. Addressing the work of a number of writers in the field of new materialism, such as Myra J. Hird and Celia Roberts (2011, 109) as well as Noela Davis (2009, 67), she notes a tendency on their part to conflate dualism with the mere act of drawing distinctions between, for instance, the human and the non-human. It is necessary, Gunnarsson asserts, to

> "discriminate between *distinction* or *difference* on one hand and *dualism* or *binary opposition* on the other. In their conventional usage [...], dualisms or binaries refer to the kind of absolute separation which ignores any interconnection and mutual constitution between the two terms in question, while distinction simply means that two things are not the same, which does not imply they can be neatly separated from one another." (2013, 14; emphasis in the original)

She adds that:

> "Indeed, if we see distinctions as such as the problem, we rid ourselves of the possibility of examining the *relation* between the two terms and one will inevitably subsume the other. [...] It is when we reject any distinction that we fall prey to reductionism, such that human practices are seen as a matter only of either the natural or the social." (Gunnarsson 2013, 14; emphasis in the original)

In Gunnarsson's view, the risk of reductionism is exemplified by a recent tendency to downplay the difference between the human and non-human (2013, 13–14) in response to their previous stark separation.

In agreement with Gunnarsson's argument, I would question whether diluting the distinction between matter and mind or materiality and discourse is a promising alternative to their binary conceptual arrangement. In this chapter I will explore that question focusing on Karen Barad's approach of agential realism (2007; see also Gunnarsson 2017, 116, 119–120). Barad argues against hardwiring distinctions such as that between nature and culture or the human and the non-human into our theorizing (2003, 827–828). This does not mean that agential realism erases differences per se. On the contrary, as Barad emphasizes, difference matters, it is of consequence: "Since different agential cuts materialize different phenomena – different marks on bodies – our intra-actions do not merely effect what we know [...]; rather, our intra-actions contribute to the differential mattering of the world" (2007, 178). But she advocates examining *how* distinctions are *generated* by apparatuses that intra-actively produce phenomena which they themselves are part of. This amounts to a genealogical inquiry which seeks to trace the production of differences that shape the world as we know it, rather than taking them for granted. For instance, Barad writes: "Refusing the anthropocentrisms of humanism and antihumanism, *posthumanism* marks the practice of accounting for the boundary-making practices by which the 'human' and its others are differentially delineated and defined" (2007, 136; emphasis in the original). However, such inquiry provides no automatic answer to the normative question of whether we should continue to maintain the relevant distinctions or not. It is this question that I raise here with reference to the distinction between matter and mind.

What is problematic about dualistic theorizing and how can we move beyond it?

Barad seems equivocal about the prospect of dissolving the distinction between matter and mind rather than merely opposing a dualistic framing of this distinction. At times she insists that materiality and discourse mutually entail each other, rather than effacing the theoretical differentiation between them. For instance, she maintains that the organism named *brittlestar* engages in discursive practices no less than do humans through "boundary-drawing practices by which it differentiates itself from the [ocean, C.B.] environment with which it intra-acts and by which it makes sense of its world, enabling it to discern a predator, for example" (2007, 375). Barad clarifies in a footnote: "This is not to suggest that materiality and discourse are therefore to be held as equivalent, but rather that the relationship is one of mutual entailment" (2007, 470, n. 44). Yet, elsewhere, she writes:

> "The separation of epistemology from ontology is a reverberation of a metaphysics *that assumes an inherent difference* [emphasis added] between human and nonhuman, subject and object, mind and body, matter and discourse. *Onto-epistem-ology* [emphasis in the original] – the study of practices of knowing in being – is probably a better way to think about the kind of understandings that are needed to come to terms with how specific intra-actions matter." (2003, 829)

This amounts to stating that there is no inherent difference between matter and discourse according to agential realism. We may ask: If we should not assume that that there is an inherent difference between matter and discourse, then in what sense is Barad maintaining that their relationship can be specified as being one of mutual entailment, rather than of equivalence or even identity? If this is to be understood as an attempt to *reconstitute* the distinction in performative, non-essentialist terms, then Barad is still theoretically ambiguous about how to specify the difference between matter and discourse. She offers a definition of "discursive practices and material phenomena and the relationship between them" as follows (2003, 828): Discursive practices are "specific material (re)configurings of the world through which local determinations of boundaries, properties and meanings are differentially enacted". Whereas matter "is substance in its intra-active becoming – not a thing but a doing, a congealing of agency" (2003, 828). These definitions blur into each other to such an extent that matter(ing)-as-doing and discursive practice become indistinguishable. Hence, it is difficult to see how a relationship between them could be specified that does not ultimately involve equating the two.

Adding to the ambiguity in Barad's writing as to how precisely (if at all) to distinguish between discourse and materiality, at times she colors the very notion of *distinction* (between these terms, along with others) in normatively negative terms. This relates to Gunnarsson's observations about a similar tendency in the work of the new materialist writers mentioned above. For instance, Barad's reading of Niels Bohr encompasses the argument that:

"Bohr's commitment to finding a way to hang on to objectivity in the face of the significant role of 'subjective elements' such as human concepts in the production of phenomena underlines his opposition to idealism and relativism. Apparatuses are not Kantian conceptual frameworks; they are physical arrangements. And phenomena do not refer merely to perception of the human mind; rather, phenomena are real physical entities or beings (though not fixed and separately delineated things). Hence I conclude that Bohr's framework is consistent with a particular notion of realism, *which is not parasitic on* subject-object, culture-nature, and word-world *distinctions*." (2007, 129; emphasis added)

While Barad is here characterizing Bohr's philosophy rather than her own, the last sentence in the above quotation does entail a normative charge of disapproval of the distinctions mentioned, as fundamental theoretical distinctions. This would seem to indicate that she finds it desirable to transcend these distinctions (see also Gunnarsson 2017, 116, 119–120).

Similarly, Barad writes of the distinction between animate and inanimate matter:

"The inanimate-animate *distinction* is perhaps one of the most persistent *dualisms* in Western philosophy and its critiques; even some of the most hard-hitting critiques of the nature-culture *dichotomy* leave the animate-inanimate *distinction* in place. It takes a radical rethinking of agency to appreciate how lively even 'dead matter' can be." (2007, 419, n. 27; emphasis added)

As in the previous quotation, here the term *distinction* carries a rather negative normative charge: Barad is in this passage clearly *critiquing* the distinction between 'animate' and 'inanimate' as such and, indeed, seems to be advocating the desirability of *overcoming* it. This would go significantly beyond advocating that we examine how the distinction has come into being.

How can we understand this tendency, manifest intermittently in Barad's work, of striving to dissolve or, at least, to blur theoretical distinctions that conventionally have been framed in dualistic terms, rather than – as stated at other points of her work – merely undertaking the investigation of their production? I suggest that we understand this tendency as a response to the problematization of dualism. In the above quotation from Barad, we may observe the same slippage between the terms *dualism* and *distinction* which Gunnarsson has identified in some other new materialist writing. Given this slippage, it is worth asking what it is about dualism that renders it problematic from a feminist perspective and what would be the most promising strategy for moving beyond the problem(s) identified. While there is probably a consensus within feminist theory that dualism is problematic, the question I have just posed has been answered in different ways by different feminists (see Butler 1990, 7–13, for a concise analysis). Therefore, discussion of appropriate ways of responding to dualism necessitates being specific about one's analysis as to precisely what makes it objectionable. Unfortunately, I find such specification to be missing both from Barad's writing and from the debate about new materialism, opened by Ahmed, to which this chapter seeks to contribute.

Hinton is the only participant in this debate to specify any reason as to why a dualistic approach to matter (in particular) should be problematic. On this subject she states:

> "[F]ar from recuperating binary terms in order to show what is at stake regarding matter, Barad urges us to consider the productive efforts of binarism at the same time that *we must concede to the im/possibility of a nature/culture dualism* in the first instance, *a claim which is made on the basis of a fundamental rethinking of the nature of difference that quantum mechanics introduces to the body of feminist theory* that engages with these questions." (2013, 180–181; emphasis added)

Why must we 'concede to the im/possibility of a nature/culture dualism'? How does quantum mechanics render such a dualism untenable? While Hinton does not answer these questions directly, her reading of Barad seems to entail an objection to dualism based ultimately upon experimental findings such as the ones Barad recounts in some detail in *Meeting the Universe Halfway* (2007). That is to say, Hinton's view is that it is because quantum mechanics as read by Barad shows the nature/culture dualism to be *empirically inaccurate* that we should strive to move beyond it in our theorizing.

By contrast, my view is that the chief problem with dualistic thinking is not the empirical inaccuracies entailed in any particular dualism, nor even the lack of theoretical complexity involved in dualistic thinking, in general (see Gunnarsson 2017). Instead, I regard the main problem with dualistic thinking as being its enmeshment with *relations of domination and exclusion*. That is, it is for ethico-political reasons first and foremost that I find the project of moving beyond dualistic discourses crucial. With this view I follow a broad line of analysis of the problematic of dualism, or of 'binary opposition' (as it was more commonly referred to at the time), that has been established within Cultural Studies in the late twentieth century in the light of deconstruction. The line of analysis I am referring to has been articulated in the 1990s within feminist and queer as well as postcolonial theory (e.g. Bhabha 1994; Butler 1990, Ch. 1; Spivak 1990), for instance. Ernesto Laclau provides a succinct elucidation of the relevant understanding as to how dualism is implicated in relations of power that are hierarchizing as well as exclusionary. He writes:

> "Derrida has shown how an identity's constitution is always based on excluding something and establishing a violent hierarchy between the two resultant poles – [...] man/woman etc. In linguistics a distinction is made between 'marked' and 'unmarked' terms. The latter convey the principal meaning of a term, while marked terms add a supplement or mark to it. [...] In this respect, we could say that the discursive construction of secondariness is based on a difference between two terms where one maintains its specificity, but where this specificity is simultaneously presented as equivalent to that which is shared by both of them. The word 'man' differentiates the latter from 'woman' but is also equated with 'human being' which is the condition shared by both men and women. What is peculiar to the second term is

thus reduced to the function of accident, as opposed to the essentiality of the first. It is the same with the black-white relationship, in which 'white', of course, is equivalent to 'human being'. 'Woman' and 'black' are thus marks, in contrast to the unmarked terms of 'man' and 'white'" (1990, 32–33).

Binary or dualistic conceptual frameworks such as the opposition man/woman thus tend to be *hierarchical* (in the sense of "unegalitarian") in virtue of privileging one of the terms as intrinsically superior. By "intrinsically superior" I mean to designate a reified form of normative evaluation, which – rather than marking the act of evaluation as such – imputes an objective superiority or inferiority to the term(s) being construed in the relevant ways (see chapter 5 for further discussion of normativity and antinormativity). This enables an essentialized standing, within hegemonic discourses, of terms such as 'man' or 'white' as putatively independent of their respective Other(s), such as 'woman' or 'black', as elucidated by Laclau in the above quotation.

As has been well-established by feminist writers of various theoretical orientations, any dualisms within Western discourses, scholarly and otherwise, are gendered in that their respective poles are coded as masculine vs. feminine (see e.g. Benjamin 1988; Bordo 1986; Flax 1993). This includes the dualisms most debated within new materialism, such as between culture and nature, discourse and materiality, as well as between the human and the non-human. Indeed, male-biased discourses tend to operate by normatively privileging whichever term in a given dualism is coded as the masculine pole in a reified form, as detailed above. This is why seeking to move beyond dualism by effacing or blurring the relevant distinctions as such runs the risk of reproducing heteronormative order by privileging either pole (whether it be the pole marked as 'masculine' or the one marked as 'feminine' within such order) – in line with Gunnarsson's argument that "if we see distinctions as such as the problem, we rid ourselves of the possibility of examining the *relation* between the two terms and one will inevitably subsume the other" (2013, 14; emphasis in the original). For instance, even if – like Barad – we undertake to move beyond the distinction between mind and matter, it may be that the conceptual outcome privileges either mind or matter in such a way that one pole is understood reductively in terms of the other. Thus, Barad (2007, 64, 151, 232) has critiqued Judith Butler's (1993) account of materiality on the grounds that it reduces the latter to an effect of culture, even as this account strives to reformulate the mind/matter relationship in a non-dualistic way. Whether such reduction occurs in a way which one-sidedly privileges mind *or* matter, we risk losing what is specific to the other term, respectively. With a view to heteronormative and male-dominated social orders, regardless of whether we efface gendered distinctions in terms that privilege the 'masculine' or the 'feminine' side of a given dualism in a manner that reifies either term as superior or intrinsically more relevant, we will have failed truly to transcend the relevant dualism. The understanding of dualism or binary opposition being detailed here sets apart *supremacist* discourses such as masculinist ones from forms of normative evaluation, as found in certain (though by no means all) feminisms, that would draw distinctions, even value-laden ones, without reifying the normative priorities involved. 'Normative' within this book is meant simply to designate any value-coded construction. I am assuming that any discursive (and thus any theoretical) practice inescapably entails a normative dimension. (See also chapters 4 and 5.)

What sense of ethics is entailed in agential realism?

If, as I have argued, the theoretical project of moving beyond dualism, in general, is best viewed as being motivated ethically and politically, then we need to ask what the *ethico-political* reason is for moving beyond the opposition between discourse and materiality, in particular. What reason does Barad give for her project of doing so? Certainly she presents agential realism as an ethical project. Thus she introduces it

> "as an epistemological-ontological-ethical framework that provides
> an understanding of the role of human *and* nonhuman, material

and discursive, and natural *and* cultural factors in scientific and other social-material practices, thereby moving such considerations beyond the well-worn debates that pit constructivism against realism, agency against structure, and idealism against materialism" (2007, 26; emphasis in the original).

What notion of ethics is entailed in this framework? It is a notion that incorporates all forms of matter into the realm of ethics. Agential realism assumes a "distribution of agency over human, nonhuman, and cyborgian forms" (2007, 218) and posits that "'we' are not the only active beings" (2007, 391). Instead, everything that partakes in the becoming of the universe is seen to be actively involved in that process. In particular, this encompasses both animate and inanimate matter, which accordingly is considered by Barad to be alive, as we saw earlier. In virtue of being "agentive" (2007, 177–178), *everything* is accountable to the specific materializations – the phenomena – of which it forms a part, as what becomes at any one moment matters for any subsequent developments (2007, 91, 178–179, 184–185, 340).

In the ethics entailed in Barad's approach, what are conventionally referred to as things or objects are thus both themselves considered accountable and are considered to form part of that to which we (humans and, specifically, scholars) are accountable. But what notion of accountability is involved here? Nowhere in her book-length exposition of agential realism does Barad (2007) elaborate what it might possibly mean either to be accountable to a thing, an object, or to consider an object accountable. In the absence of any such explanation, I would insist that the notion of ethics makes sense only in relation to subjects – understood, not in a humanist sense but, instead, as encompassing all that is capable of experience, and therefore, of suffering. It is the possibility of their suffering that makes us responsible to sentient beings in particular. It is this possibility that makes it wrong to relate to subjects in the stated sense as if they were objects. By contrast, to feel responsible or accountable to what can be affected ontologically but not experientially – for instance, when being destroyed – seems to me to involve a projection of the said feature of subjectivity onto objects, understood along these lines as what does not care, even about 'its own' becoming or unbecoming.

To be sure, the question can be raised as to how we can be certain that any matter exists which is purely object in this sense. It is not my purpose to preclude from ethical consideration what is conventionally referred to as inanimate, non-living matter. My purpose instead is to defend an understanding of ethics as being tied by definition to vulnerability. Such an understanding emerges, for instance, from Butler's work (2004a; 2005; 2010), which for this very reason can be considered as posing a challenge to the ethics formulated by Barad. Butler has repeatedly critiqued forms of politics (particularly by the U.S.) that exploit the fact that subjects are exposed to one another in ways they cannot fully control, along with the fact that vulnerability is distributed highly unevenly across the globe (e.g. 2004a, 28–32). Her theorization of the subject emphasizes these particular features of what she refers to as "[p]recarious [l]ife" (2004a, title; emphasis added). We can derive from her work a notion of ethics according to which ethical striving responds to a concern to minimize suffering of any kind, to avoid contributing to its coming-about or aggravation as far as possible, and to struggle for the achievement and sustenance of conditions in which the *needs* of sentient beings are taken care of, such that they may live or even thrive rather than merely survive (cf. Butler 2012a, 15) or even die.

My disagreement with Barad, then, does not turn on the fact that she questions the distinction between animate and inanimate matter per se. Instead it concerns the *grounds* on which she views 'dead matter' as alive. Whereas I consider the capacity for experience to be definitive of life as relevant to ethical consideration – *whether or not this encompasses all forms of matter* – such capacity seems not to figure in Barad's understanding of life, nor of ethics. Instead, life, as well as accountability, in her view seem to be defined in terms of the agentive role (e.g. Barad 2007, 177–178) which she attributes to all matter, whether conventionally viewed as 'animate' or 'inanimate'. Thus agency in her account "is not aligned with human intentionality or subjectivity" (Barad 2007, 177). Rather, "agency is the space of

possibilities opened up by the indeterminacies entailed in exclusions"
(2007, 182) – exclusions as constitutive of all materialization according
to her (2007, 177, 393–394). Barad frames agency in terms of an
enactment (2007, 178) rather than an attribute (2007, 141). It appears
to be its active involvement in the becoming of the universe, then, that
makes 'dead matter' alive in her view. Accordingly, she asserts that:
"There is a vitality to the liveliness of intra-activity, not in the sense of
a new form of vitalism, but rather in terms of a new sense of aliveness"
(2007, 177). In a footnote she adds: "This new sense of aliveness applies
to the inanimate as well as the animate, or rather, it is what makes
possible the very distinction between the animate and the inanimate"
(2007, 437, n. 81). Just what it is that endows this aliveness with *ethical*
significance remains unclear, however.

I would argue, then, that the criterion whereby Barad frames life
and – seemingly as a result – accountability as encompassing all forms
of matter fails to provide a convincing reason for her incorporation of all
matter into the sphere of ethics. She thus neglects to specify an ethical
or political reason for the project of moving beyond the dualisms of
animate/inanimate matter and of matter/mind. A plausible ground for
seeking to do so in my view is that we cannot rule out the possibility
that all matter is sentient in some sense. Yet, as I have pointed out, the
capacity for experience in virtue of which sentient being is exposed to
the possibility of suffering does not figure in Barad's theory. Instead,
it is only the capacity of all matter for activity that accounts for the
liveliness which Barad attributes to all matter, including inanimate
matter.

'Merely passive'?

In fact, *passivity* is a quality that is strangely devalued by Barad. This
devaluation is entailed in the argument upon which she bases her
entire theoretical approach: the argument that matter, like mind (or
derivatively, discourse, culture and so on), is active and not passive.
Thus she writes:

"Nature is neither a passive surface awaiting the mark of culture nor the end product of cultural performances. The belief that nature is mute and immutable and that all prospects for significance and change reside in culture is a reinscription of the nature/culture dualism that feminists have actively contested." (2003, 827)

"For all Foucault's emphasis on the political anatomy of disciplinary power, he too fails to offer an account of the body's historicity in which its very materiality plays an *active* role in the workings of power. This implicit reinscription of matter's passivity is a mark of extant elements of representationalism that haunt his largely post-representationalist account." (2003, 809; emphasis in the original)

Barad's devaluation of passivity accords with hegemonic, male-supremacist[1] discourse, which feminizes that attribute. This forms a case in point illustrating my earlier argument that to seek to transcend dualism by eliding distinctions does not necessarily rescue us from reproducing the hierarchical arrangement underpinning the opposition concerned. Thus, it would seem in this instance that declaring nature or matter to be just as active, or similarly active, as culture or mind – a declaration found in new materialism more generally and articulated much earlier by Donna Haraway[2] – reinforces the privilege which activity tends to be accorded vis-à-vis passivity within masculinist discourses. This is to seek to undo one gendered opposition by reinforcing another one.

This attempt is all the less felicitous as a feminist political strategy considering that passivity is a constitutive dimension of experience. It is by virtue of their exposure to what is beyond their control that sentient beings are exposed to the possibility of suffering. I make this claim, again, with Butler's theorizing in mind, which emphasizes our simultaneous formation by, and subjection to, power *along with*

---

1   I borrow this term from Nancy Fraser (2013, 9).
2   See Haraway (1991, 197–200) as well as Alaimo and Hekman (2008, 4–7); Bennett (2010, esp. 34); Coole and Frost (2010, 8–9); Davis (2009, 73); Hird (2004, 228); Kirby (2011, 66).

the (limited) agency that is generated in virtue of the constitution of subjects.[3] When she writes of our exposure to violence, for instance, she emphasizes not solely our responsibility in the face of this (2004a, 16) but – simultaneously – the de-constituting force we are subject to:

> "Violence is surely a touch of the worst order, a way a primary human vulnerability to other humans is exposed in its most terrifying way, a way in which we are given over, without control, to the will of another, a way in which life itself can be expunged by the willful action of another." (2004a, 28–29)

It is with a view to such a sense of being 'given over, without control' that I am suggesting that to be exposed to experiences we cannot (fully) choose lends a dimension of passivity to the very capacity for experience – a dimension that is prominent in the vulnerability which Butler proposes humans share (2004a, Ch. 2).

Passivity in this sense may be traumatic, but there is no reason to *devalue* it in terms of a discourse that would position it as inferior vis-à-vis activity. Rather than privileging the latter term over the former, and rather than dichotomizing both qualities against each other (as in the suggestion that all that exists is essentially active *rather than* passive), it should be possible to recognize both, in non-dualistic and non-hierarchizing terms, as forming features of sentient existence.

I would argue, in fact, that unless we question the hierarchical opposition active/passive (as instantiated in Barad's discourse), it will be impossible fully to extricate matter from its hierarchical opposition to mind. For, as Barad also implies, it is *in virtue of* the attribution of 'mere passivity' (as a negative attribution) to matter that the latter historically has been devalued. Yet her strategy of argument effectively amounts to reinscribing in a reified form the normative privilege which activity and agency have historically been accorded vis-à-vis passivity. This is the case inasmuch as nowhere in *Meeting the Universe Halfway* (2007) does she justify or even recognize the fact that the argument

---

3   See esp. Butler (2015b, 14–16); cf. note 11 to this chapter.

upon which she bases her theoretical approach, as paraphrased above, accords more value to activity than to passivity.

In my own analysis, the rationale based on which matter has historically been devalued vis-à-vis mind is that matter, being merely passive, is *mere object*. As Barad seems to agree, subjectivity in Western discursive convention has often been defined over and against 'mere objects' – or 'mere matter', as she would be more likely to put it – as superior in virtue of being associated with activity and agency. This, I would argue, forms the essence of the subject/object dualism which is so fundamental to the hierarchical set-up in which difference is thought in much hegemonic discourse:[4] The category 'object' within Western-style theorizing has figured as Other[5] or as the constitutive outside[6] to the category 'subject' – a term which has tended to be reserved for human beings.

As a feminist, I consider to be fundamentally problematic and unconvincing the association of the status of subject with an agency or activity defined over and against the passivity associated with 'mere objects' (or 'mere matter') – albeit on different grounds than Barad's. Rather than seeking to recognize the agentive capacity of matter, thus expanding the notions of agency and activity to apply to all that exists, I find it ethically necessary to ask the following questions: On what grounds is passivity inferiorized, i.e. culturally disregarded, in the Western imagination? What kind of discursive logic and what ethico-politics are entailed in defining subjects' imputed difference from, and superiority to, objects in terms that identify the latter with an abjected passivity? And why would passivity be attributed to *objects* or matter more readily than to subjects, as Barad suggests? Are passivity and the predicament of being exposed to the doings of subjects or other forces particular to objects? Obviously not.

I propose that, instead, the masculinist, bourgeois, Eurocentric subject of Western philosophy (understood in the sense of a discursive

---

4   See e.g. Benjamin (1988); Ferguson (1993).
5   Cf. Spivak (1985, 247).
6   Cf. Butler (1993, 3).

position of subjectivity) arrives at considering himself a subject *on the basis of* abjecting passivity as Other. The category 'object' figures as a screen or receptacle for Man's projection of his own sense of vulnerability, which he disavows. Objects are thus defined as what the subject 'is not', i.e. does not wish to be. Inferiorizing passivity seems to hark back to a discursive logic whereby to be active *rather than* passive – that is, to polarize both attributes against one another whilst equating one term with 'self' and negating its counterpart – is to assign superior value to a 'subject' *on grounds of his self-imputed strength or power to act*; in binary opposition to what is exposed *to* the actions of others. Passivity here seems to be coded in terms of weakness and vulnerability – an exposure, ultimately, to *others'* power or agency. The widespread association of patriarchy, racism and other (intersecting) systems of domination with an *objectification* of subjects would seem to make sense in terms of this discursive logic, that is, in terms of the idea that to be a subject is to be worth more than an object *because one is capable of activity or has 'agency'* (which endowment these systems of domination disavow in their respective Others).

In order to undo the subject/object dualism, thus understood, it is necessary to take account of subjects' exposure to what they cannot control,[7] and hence, of the capacity for experience which is constitutive of the vulnerability that comes with being a subject. This is irrespective of whether this category is taken to have an empirical counterpart, that is, of whether any such thing as a pure 'object', devoid of experience, actually exists. It is only on account of an empathy with what might possibly suffer that ethical concern makes sense.[8]

---

7   Cf. Butler (2004a; 2005; 2010).

8   Cf. Puig de la Bellacasa (2010, 158–159). Much as empathy is often invoked in politically problematic ways that sustain rather than disrupt social inequality (Berlant 2004; Pedwell 2012a, 2012b, 2013), and so is by no means necessarily ethical, I would maintain that ethics cannot do without empathy, in the sense that a refusal of empathy in many cases negates the possibility of an ethical practice. I follow Butler in emphasizing the destructive and potentially deadly effects of refused identification (1997, 137, 148–149; 2009, 78, 92) as well as – by extension – of refused empathy. As Carolyn Pedwell notes, empathy is closely

Subjectivity beyond the subject/object dualism

For the above reasons, it would seem to be impossible to overcome the mind/matter dualism unless we reframe the notion of subjectivity in a way consonant with the concern to include within this category all that might possibly be exposed to suffering – that is, in a way which acknowledges subjects' passive exposure to what is beyond their control as definitive of their predicament. By the same token, it is by disentangling the notion of passivity from its displacement onto objects and, thus, onto matter (especially inanimate matter) that these latter concepts can be extricated from the reified, hierarchical opposition of subject vs. object in which they historically have been framed, as I have argued. When we conceive of subjectivity inclusively in terms of *all* sentient being's exposure to experience, and thus to the possibility of suffering, this term would itself seem no longer to be defined by a subject/object dualism that (as analyzed in the previous section) makes for a *supremacist notion* of subjectivity as essentially superior to objects. I see no necessary reason why subjectivity would require the notion of object as its counterpart, even though I do not in principle oppose the possibility of retaining the category of object for forms of matter – which may or may not exist – that might be established in some sense to be non-sentient. Even if such a category were retained, on

---

associated with identification (2012b, 282). The notion of refused identification can thus alert us to the selectivity with which empathy is extended to certain subjects while being refused others. To be refused identification and empathy is, on this understanding, to be consigned to the status of the unintelligible; of the "less than human" (Butler 2004b, 218) or – as I prefer to put it in less anthropocentric terms – of 'life unworthy of life'. As such, the systematic refusal of empathy to certain groups of living beings is associated with biopolitical dividing practices that would differentiate between beings 'worthy of life' vs. those considered, in the most extreme case, "killable" (Haraway 2008, 75–79). I suggest that an ethico-political assessment of empathy should turn on whether its specific articulation and mode of operation in any one context tends more towards stabilizing or towards challenging relations of inequality and domination, both of which are possible scenarios.

this understanding it would no longer be inferiorized as subjectivity's Other.

This is what differentiates a *hierarchical opposition* enmeshed in relations of domination and exclusion from a *distinction* which turns on a criterion unrelated to notions of an intrinsic superiority vs. inferiority: The subject/object dualism as elucidated in the previous section operates according to a normative logic that, in imputing superior value to what is capable of activity as compared to what (supposedly) is not, is both masculinist and – ultimately – biopolitical. I here use the term "biopolitical" in the sense that different forms of life or 'dead matter' are hierarchically ranked in terms of their imputed *value* (cf. Butler 2012a, 10). This is in contrast with a notion of subjects which – if distinguished from objects at all – turns on a need for protection that is derived, not from any notion of value or *worthiness* of protection but, instead, from subjects' capacity for suffering. In the latter case, what is at work is an ethics based on need and not on a notion of worth.

The account of matter upon which Barad bases her argument that matter merits scholarly attention and recognition by feminists seems to mimic the supremacist logic which I have problematized as being masculinist and biopolitical.[9] Consider the following two statements by her:

---

9   I would note that to analyze a given practice as masculinist, biopolitical or, indeed, as dualistic does not automatically amount to engaging in a dualistic practice oneself. Whereas I have been analyzing Barad's theoretical discourse as masculinist in its reifying devaluation of passivity – which it shares with other masculinist discourses that put to work a dualistic distinction between *active* and *passive* – my own normative distinction between masculinist and feminist discourse abstains from promoting as superior either what is conventionally masculinized or feminized. Instead I seek to engage in a form of feminist practice that self-consciously prioritizes an egalitarian and non-reifying mode of normativity (see chapter 5 for more detail), along with a relational form of analysis. By this I mean that, rather than treating either term in any conceptual pair as self-sufficient and intrinsically superior – a characteristic of dualism as analyzed earlier – I seek to treat both sides of the relevant distinction in terms of a *relationship* in which one term features as the dominant one, without either maintaining or inverting the hierarchy involved.

"By 'posthumanist' I mean to signal the crucial recognition that nonhumans play an important role in naturalcultural practices, including everyday social practices, scientific practices, and practices that do not include humans." (Barad 2007, 32)

"Crucial to understanding the workings of power is an understanding of the nature of power in the fullness of its materiality. To restrict power's productivity to the limited domain of the 'social,' for example, or to figure matter as merely an end product rather than an active factor in further materializations, *is to cheat matter out of the fullness of its capacity*." (Barad 2003, 810; emphasis added)

In the latter quotation, power is equated with capacity – the capacity that Barad finds us at risk of cheating matter out of – in a way which celebrates the capacity or power of matter as worthy and meriting recognition, if not admiration. I find Barad's apparent admiration for the capacity or power of matter to resonate uneasily with biopolitical discursive logics that would base recognition vs. a refusal of recognition upon judgments regarding a putative intrinsic value of life, as elucidated above. In contrast with a notion of life as intrinsically valuable or as devoid of specific value, I would assert that *vulnerability* is what is in need of recognition – a form of recognition that is discursively aligned with a concern to protect, rather than with admiration for strength.[10]

Similarly, with reference to the first of the two quotations above, would not recognizing matter for its important role in naturalcultural practices merely entail the extension to 'creation' as a whole of the colonialist logic of hierarchizing against each other capacities – and, thus, the beings with which they are associated – in terms of their

---

10 The notion of protection, while it potentially incorporates that of self-protection, nonetheless may involve a paternalistic distinction between what protects and what will be protected. I cannot address this problem within the scope of this book, but I suggest that the ethical necessity of protecting precarious lives (cf. Butler 2004a) is not obviated by the potential for paternalistic domination which is raised by asserting such necessity.

supposed contribution to 'civilization'? It would seem preferable that we, as subjects of theoretical discourse as much as of practical politics, should strive to leave behind the very logic of assigning importance to entities or forces based on their contribution to naturalcultural – or indeed to any – practices. Such logic would seem, problematically, to be indebted to the liberal notion of 'merit' and its flipside: the notion of 'life unworthy of life'. Moreover, extending the notion of merit from its conventional application to human subjects to apply to nature as a whole would amount to anthropomorphizing the latter.

Conclusion

I have argued that Barad's tendency – at least intermittently – to dilute the distinction between matter and mind (along with that between animate and inanimate matter), or to color such distinctions in normatively negative terms, falls short of accomplishing what is needed in order to overcome the hierarchical character of the dualisms of subject vs. object and, by extension, of matter vs. mind. Agential realism fails to challenge the hierarchical conceptual arrangement based on which matter historically has been construed as inferior to mind or the human subject. It does not tackle the devaluation of passivity which has been problematically associated with matter or objects more readily than with mind or subjects. If we want to disentangle these notions from the hierarchizing thrust which they acquire when framed in terms of the subject/object dualism, we need to target the reified character of the active/passive opposition which accounts for the inferiorization of both 'objects' and 'matter'.

As I have suggested, we can do so by reconceptualizing subjectivity in non-hierarchizing terms. There would be no need, then, to abandon the distinctions either between subjects and objects or between mind and matter in order to extricate these notions from hierarchical thinking and its implication in unegalitarian social orders. Moreover, the abandonment of either of these distinctions would not necessarily achieve that goal. On the contrary, as I have argued, effacing or blurring distinctions does not necessarily eliminate the hierarchical framing that binary oppositions tend to entail. As noted above, Barad's strategy of highlighting the agentive role of all matter comes at the cost of continuing the devaluation of passivity. As a result, the ethical rationale for moving beyond the dichotomy between mind and matter in the first place remains obscure: What is to be gained by this undertaking if the underlying hierarchy is left intact?

In line with Gunnarsson's argument elucidated earlier, I contend that reconceptualizing matter and mind in non-hierarchizing, non-dualistic ways might involve exploring other ways of relating these terms to one another than either opposing or mutually assimilating them. Arguably, Barad opts for the latter possibility in highlighting matter's and mind's shared agentive role. However, this may obscure or elide important differences between the senses in which various forms of matter and mind, respectively, might be agentive. For instance, it is not clear that all matter is agentive in a sense associated with an ability to be held accountable. Even if matter were accountable, there remains the problem of how we conceive of such accountability and whether we are using this term in the same sense we do in referring to adult human beings as accountable. We must consider that there may be quite different senses of the terms 'agency' and 'accountability' at work in these respective contexts. Rather than eliding the differences between these, as a corollary of eliding the distinction between mind and matter, I suggest that a more promising strategy would move beyond a dualistic framing of this distinction by opening up different meanings of 'activity' as well as 'passivity' in contexts involving different forms of matter and mind.[11]

---

11   For instance, subject formation and its imbrication with material supports would seem to involve passivity and activity on either side – both the side of the emerging subject and that of "technologies, structures, institutions" (and much else) that forms part of the "conditions of emergence" of a subject (Butler 2015b, 14). As Butler puts it, "[a] support must *support*, and so both be and act" (Butler 2015b, 14; emphasis in the original). Likewise, she writes of the "localized field of impressionability" that is the emerging subject that it is "[a]cted on, animated, and acting; addressed, animated, and addressing;

Overall, I highlight the risk of negating or understating differences which is involved in striving to overcome dualism by emphasizing sameness or similarity. There is a reductionism entailed in this, which Gunnarsson (2013) has pointed out. Moreover, from an ethical perspective, this could be an assimilatory move that may well underestimate power differentials in the rather different senses of 'agency'.[12] Considering adult human agency as qualitatively different from other kinds of agency may mean marking human *privilege* rather than a fictive human superiority. Such privilege is easily erased from view by the new materialist emphasis upon likeness or similarity (between human and non-human, culture and nature, animate and inanimate) at the cost of giving due attention to specificity and difference.

---

touched, animated, and now sensing. These triads are partially sequential and partially chiasmic" (Butler 2015b, 14–15). Yet the simultaneous involvement of activity and passivity on both sides of this connection does not necessarily mean that inanimate supports, such as the materials with which a baby is cleaned, fed, etc., are either active (crying, smiling, etc.) or passive (impressionable) in the same sense as either the baby or its caretakers are.

12   This is illustrated by the neglect of such power differentials, and of different degrees of *mutual* engagement, in the following statements by Barad: "'Humans' and 'brittlestars' learn about and co-constitute each other through a variety of brittlestar-human intra-actions" (2007, 381–382). "As we entertain the possibilities for forming partnerships with brittlestars and other organisms for biomimetic projects, we are co-constituting ourselves into assemblages that 'mimic' (but do not replicate) the entanglements of the objects we study and the tools that we make" (2007, 383).

2 Ontology/Epistemology
Guarding Against Collapsing (Their) Difference *or* Producing a Dichotomy
Or: Between and Beyond Antonio Negri, Michael Hardt, Karen Barad and Dennis Bruining

Introduction

In 2005 Clare Hemmings published a critique of certain writings related to the "ontological turn" in the journal *Cultural Studies*. According to her, some cultural theorists – such as Brian Massumi and Eve Kosofsky Sedgwick – tend to construct earlier poststructuralist theorizing as overwhelmingly 'negative' and totalizing in its view of power as an all-pervasive constituent of sociality. As a supposed remedy against what they portray as the socially determinist bias of earlier poststructuralisms, these authors according to Hemmings celebrate affect as "'the new cutting edge'" (Hemmings 2005, 548 [Abstract]) in a way that, as she argues, tends to severe affect from sociality. Authors associated with the recent turn to affect "emphasize the unexpected, the singular, or indeed the quirky, over the generally applicable, where the latter becomes associated with the pessimism of social determinist perspectives, and the former with the hope of freedom from social constraint" (Hemmings 2005, 550).

What is important for my purposes here is that Hemmings charges the writers I have mentioned with producing almost a duality between existing poststructuralist theory and what they propose as the way forward – a dichotomy in which 'epistemology' and 'ontology' are polarized against one another. Thus, she writes: "Part of what makes critical theory so uninventive for Sedgwick is its privileging of the epistemological, since a relentless attention to the structures of truth and knowledge obscures our experience of those structures. She advocates instead a reparative return to the ontological and intersubjective, to the surprising and enlivening texture of individuality and community" (Hemmings 2005, 553). Hemmings polemicizes: "the 'problem of epistemology' only materializes in the moment that it is chronologically and intellectually separated from ontology. Ontology thus resolves the problem its advocates invent" (2005, 557). Further, she argues that "[p]ositing affect as a 'way out' *requires* that poststructuralist epistemology have ignored embodiment, investment and emotion" (2005, 556–557; emphasis in the original). This is not the case, as Hemmings insists, by reference to postcolonial theorists, amongst others (2005, 558). Yet, as she maintains, their work *needs* to be omitted from accounts of the supposedly miserable state of Cultural Studies *in order* for affect studies to be positioned as singular in its attention to the body and the affective. In this way, "affective rewriting flattens out poststructuralist inquiry by ignoring the counter-hegemonic contributions of postcolonial and feminist theorists, only thereby positioning affect as 'the answer' to contemporary problems of cultural theory" (2005, 548 [Abstract]).

While I disagree with Hemmings to the extent that, in my view, affectivity has indeed been neglected in much early poststructuralist theorizing – especially in classical instances of such theorizing, such as Michel Foucault's work – I want to take up Hemmings' critical observations as to a recent tendency to produce a dichotomy between ontology and epistemology. It is thus the ontological turn that I am concerned with in this chapter, to the extent that it can be distinguished from (much as it is related to) the affective turn, which I will address in detail in chapter 3.

One irony of the recent turn from the epistemological emphasis of twentieth-century poststructuralism to the ontological emphasis associated with the widespread turn to Gilles Deleuze's philosophy within progressive cultural and social analysis is that it risks being oblivious to a critique of Deleuze (along with Foucault) which Gayatri Chakravorty Spivak articulated in her seminal essay, "Can the Subaltern Speak?", as early on as in the 1980s. I want to return to this essay, along with further early work by Spivak, as a way of placing in perspective 'the ontological turn' in its neglect of 'epistemology' – as much as any inverse move. Commenting upon a published conversation between Deleuze and Foucault (1980), held in 1972, Spivak in "Can the Subaltern Speak?" chided both writers for "an unquestioned valorization of the oppressed as subject" (1988a, 274; see also Spivak 1988a, 278). As one example of what she wished to problematize, she mentioned Foucault's remark that "'the masses *know* perfectly well, clearly' [...] 'they know far better than [the intellectual, G.C.S.] and they certainly say it very well'" (cited in Spivak 1988a, 274; emphasis in the original). She comments: "What happens to the critique of the sovereign subject in these pronouncements?" (Spivak 1988a, 274), adding: "The banality of leftist intellectuals' list of self-knowing, politically canny subalterns stands revealed; representing them, the intellectuals represent themselves as transparent" (1988a, 275).

In my reading, Spivak in the essay "Can the Subaltern Speak?" posits that for intellectuals situated in the academies of the global North to make utterances such as the one just cited is to disavow their own role in representing the subaltern. This is to abdicate, as I understand Spivak, a responsibility which she attributes to intellectuals so positioned, of producing discourses that self-consciously attend to global power differentials and to their own positions within global hierarchies (see Spivak 1988a, 279–280). She thus seems to advocate for a strategy of representation whereby intellectuals represent other subjects – especially subaltern subjects – explicitly *in their own name*, thus acknowledging their own mediating role, and their inescapable power of representation, as intellectuals.

The link between these two forms of politics with primarily epistemological vs. primarily ontological concerns is implicitly made by Spivak in the same essay when, critiquing a statement by Deleuze according to which "[r]eality is what actually happens in a factory, in a school, in baracks, in a prison, in a police station" (cited in Spivak 1988a, 275), she asserts that "[this foreclosing of the necessity of the difficult task of counterhegemonic ideological production] has helped positivist empiricism – the justifying foundation of advanced capitalist neocolonialism – to define its own arena as 'concrete experience', 'what actually happens'" (Spivak 1988a, 275). I read Spivak as positing by this statement that an empiricist insistence that we have unmediated access to an ontological 'nature of things' is complicit with (neo-)colonial discourses *in virtue of* its dismissal of the epistemological notion of mediation. I take it that what she means by this amounts to the discourse-theoretical point that proclamations to the effect that 'the facts speak for themselves', rather than being inescapably enmeshed in and, indeed, rendered subject to perception in the first place by discourses – in other words, by their constitution in terms of a normatively loaded (and hence, power-charged) conceptual frame – disavow the inextricable link between knowledge and power. Thus she insists in the same essay that: "Representation has not withered away." (1988a, 308)

Whether one states that 'reality is what actually happens' or makes a claim to the effect that 'the oppressed know exactly what they are doing and saying' (see Spivak 1988a, 278–279): in either case the enunciating subject *is* in fact producing a particular theoretical rendering of 'reality' and of other subjects, respectively. But the mediating character of the construction concerned risks being obscured through the appeal made by each of these statements to a supposed ontological given. Thus, the very assertion that '[the masses, C.B.] know far better than [the intellectual, G.C.S.]' entails a specific rendering of subjectivity that not only disavows the intellectual's mediating role, but also posits that subjects (or at least 'the masses') are self-transparent (see also Birla 2010, 90–92). As Spivak has indicated elsewhere, the latter assumption is not necessarily a sign of respect. On the contrary, as she points out in an interview:

"If one looks at the history of post-Enlightenment theory, the major
problem has been the problem of autobiography: How subjective
structures can, in fact, give objective truth. During these same
centuries, the Native Informant [...], his stuff was unquestioningly
treated as the objective evidence for the founding of so-called sciences
like ethnography, ethno-linguistics, comparative religion, and so on.
So that, once again, the theoretical problems only relate to the person
who knows. The person who *knows* has all of the problems of selfhood.
The person who is *known*, somehow seems not to have a problematic
self" (1990, 66; emphasis in the original).

The risk of neglecting epistemological concerns is, as I read Spivak, that
those dimensions of power relations which are entailed in knowledge
production – including all academic work – are understated, if not
obscured. To be sure, post-Deleuzian ontology or at least Deleuze's
own ontology is not epistemologically naïve. As Todd May reconstructs
Deleuze's stance on the matter, practicing ontology is self-consciously
to *create* the world in novel ways rather than solely to *represent* what there
is (2005, 15–23). Yet, the political effect of Deleuzian empiricism – a
"transcendental empiricism" (Patton 2000, 40) – may be said to amount
to much the same, as is highlighted by Spivak's critique of Deleuze to
the effect that statements such as 'reality is what actually happens' write
the constituting subject (or, more precisely, the discourses in terms of
which the subject is constituted) out of the ontology he or she produces.

This becomes especially problematic in my view when Deleuze, as
much as certain followers of his, romanticizes those whom he associates
with the category of the minoritarian – from prisoners (see Deleuze in
Deleuze/Foucault 1980, *passim*) and migrants (Hardt/Negri, see below)
through to animals (critically: Haraway 2008, 27–30) – as spearheads of
revolutionary change. At an abstract level, this tendency is exemplified
by the following statement, made by Deleuze during the conversation
with Foucault which Spivak comments upon in "Can the Subaltern
Speak?":

"This is why the notion of reform is so stupid and hypocritical. Either
reforms are designed by people who claim to be representative, who

make a profession of speaking for others, and they lead to a division of power, to a distribution of this new power which is consequently increased by a double repression; or they arise from the complaints and demands of *those concerned. This latter instance is no longer a reform but revolutionary action that questions (expressing the full force of its partiality) the totality of power and the hierarchy that maintains it*" (in Deleuze/Foucault 1980, 208–209; emphasis added).

The claim that as soon as 'those concerned' speak for themselves, their actions and discourses will necessarily be revolutionary in thrust – rather than potentially 'reformist', as Deleuze implies here, or as we might also put it: rather than potentially reproducing hegemonic discourses at least in part – this claim is extremely generalizing. I, for one, find it patronizing to glorify resisting subjects in this way.

I feel the same way about the manner in which Antonio Negri and Michael Hardt – two current theorists who draw strongly upon Deleuzian philosophy – romanticize the poor and, especially, migrants as subjects of resistance. They assert that the poor, in general, and migrants, in particular – two categories which they treat as superimposable, ignoring the intersectionality of relations of domination – not only form part of the "multitude" but are particularly representative of it in virtue of their "wealth, productivity, and commonality" (Hardt/Negri 2004, 136). The poor as well as migrants come across as an avant-garde of sorts when Hardt and Negri write: "In the inferno of poverty and the odyssey of migration we have already begun to see emerge some of the outlines of the figure of the multitude" (2004, 138); a multitude which their work is bent on calling into being. In this context they assert that: "Migrants may often travel empty-handed in conditions of extreme poverty, but even then they are full of knowledges, languages, skills, and creative capacities: each migrant brings with him or her an entire world" (2004, 133). Who *doesn't* bring with him or her an entire world? Everyone does, and so this statement seems to me to engage in an idealization which romanticizes migrants as a class in a way that is devoid of substantive content. When Hardt and Negri state that "the immigrants invest the entire society with their subversive desires" (2004, 134), I find it appropriate to juxtapose this assertion with the following observation by bell hooks concerning a certain postmodern, exoticist romanticization and eroticization of 'the primitive' that, in U.S. mainstream culture, had established itself in the late twentieth century. This quotation is from her essay "Eating the Other", first published in 1992: "The contemporary crises of identity in the west, especially as experienced by white youth, are eased when the 'primitive' is recouped *via* a focus on diversity and pluralism which suggests the Other can provide life-sustaining alternatives" (hooks 2006, 369). Hooks in this text identifies as such the notion "that non-white people [have] more life experience" (2006, 368), arguing with reference to hegemonic, white subjects that "[g]etting a bit of the Other" is "considered a ritual of transcendence, a movement out into a world of difference that would transform, an acceptable rite of passage" (2006, 368) with the objective "to be changed in some way by the encounter" (2006, 368). As she explains: "Whereas mournful imperialist nostalgia constitutes the betrayed and abandoned world of the Other as an accumulation of lack and loss, contemporary longing for the 'primitive' is expressed by the projection onto the Other of a sense of plenty, bounty, a field of dreams" (2006, 369). In other words, the notion of immigrants' 'subversive desires' in Hardt's and Negri's text may well be read as a *displacement* of desire for 'the Other' – be it an exhaustively political kind of desire, or a kind that carries additional connotations – invested *by the author-subjects* in 'immigrants', who are thereby reduced to a projection screen. I want to stress, then, the colonizing thrust of Negri's and Hardt's rhetoric, as quoted above. It resonates with Deleuze's idealization of 'those concerned', i.e., of subjects engaged in resisting their own oppression (see above). Hardt's and Negri's rhetoric regarding the 'richness' of migrants, and the "subversive desires" which they attribute to 'immigrants' as a homogenized class, is no less patronizing. It reinscribes racialized discourse – which (as clarified by hooks) is no less problematic when it comes in an idealizing, exoticizing guise than it is when it is overtly devaluing.

Encarnación Gutiérrez Rodríguez aptly phrases the more general point I want to make in regard to Negri and Hardt when she critiques them, along with some of their followers, for defining the empirical faces of resistance out of existence through the abstract character of their concept of a 'multitude':

> "A *multitude* which does not pose the concrete questions pertaining to material distribution, to the aporias between North and South, the gendered subalterns, the underprivileged queers, fails to recognize [the speakers', C.B.] own possible positions of hegemonic speech, qua intellectuals or academics of the West, as a structural moment in the constitution of the *multitude*" (2007, 137; transl. C.B.; emphasis in the original).

In summary, practicing ontology or a theorization of (social) reality – especially when this occurs without any simultaneous attention to questions of epistemology or the politics of knowledge – bears the risk of facilitating the production of colonialist effects in virtue of purporting to capture a truth or reality 'beyond discourse', which is to disavow (whether explicitly or implicitly) the constitutive role of discourses; including one's own.

Ontology *versus* epistemology? Onto-epistem-ology?

As can be gleaned from the above statement by Gutiérrez Rodríguez, some *postcolonial* poststructuralisms (in particular) have never been purely about an epistemological or discursive perspective. Among the best-known postcolonial critics of the late twentieth century – Homi K. Bhabha, Edward Said and Spivak – the latter, in particular, has put deconstruction to rather materialist uses: From the 1980s onwards, her work barely, if ever left questions of ontology wholly to the side, implicated as they are in analyses of (global) social relations. After all, Spivak once called herself a "'practical deconstructivist feminist Marxist'" (as cited by her interviewer; see Spivak 1990, 133). Her eclectic way of articulating materialist with deconstructive critique bears out Hemmings' point that it would flatten out poststructuralism to reduce it to a pursuit of epistemological questions in isolation from ontological ones.

So how can we relate ontological and epistemological concerns to each other in less reductive ways? It is on this question that I want to focus in the remainder of this chapter. My central thesis in doing so – by way of juxtaposing the examples of Negri and Hardt as well as Karen Barad with some theses propounded by Spivak during the early phase of her work – is that the latter situated itself at an equal remove from, on the one hand, dichotomizing epistemology vs. ontology against each other and, on the other hand, from any attempt to reconcile epistemological with ontological concerns in an overarching theoretical framework. Spivak in my reading, at the time at least, treated epistemic and ontic aspects of sociality as being mutually imbricated yet irreducible to one another and, more precisely, as existing in mutual tension. I contrast this view as I reconstruct it favorably with, firstly, Negri's and Hardt's polarization of deconstruction and ontology against each other and, secondly, Barad's project of fusing epistemology with ontology. My basis for reconstructing Spivak's position during the 1980s is the collection of interviews with her that appeared in 1990 under the title *The Post-Colonial Critic*.

Consider how Spivak frames the relationship between textuality and "'fact' or 'life' or even 'practice'" in the following passage (from which I omit some parts) in one of those interviews:

> "As far as I understand it, the notion of textuality should be related to the notion of the worlding of a world [...] Textuality in its own way marks the place where the production of discourse [...] escapes the person or collectivity that engages in practice [...]. From this point of view, what a notion of textuality in general does is to see that what is defined over against 'The Text' as 'fact' or 'life' or even 'practice' is to an extent worlded in a certain way so that practice can take place. [...] It allows a check on the inevitable power dispersal within practice because it notices that the privileging of practice is in fact no less dangerous than the vanguardism of theory. When one says 'writing', it means this kind of structuring of the limits of the power of practice,

knowing that what is beyond practice is always organizing practice" (1990, 1–2).

As I read this passage, it is not possible according to Spivak at the same time to *engage* in a given practice and to fully *comprehend* how it is constituted in specific ways that have a textual dimension – in virtue, for instance, of the practice in question basing itself in certain presuppositions of which the subject concerned, whether individual or collective, is not fully aware. The implicit ontologies entailed in our practices are discursively constituted, then, and Spivak treats the discursive dimension of practices in such a way as to accentuate its fictional and, hence, in a certain sense arbitrary character. Arbitrary, as I would suggest, in the sense that possible alternative renderings of "'fact' or 'life' or even 'practice'" – as formulated by her in the above quotation – are excluded by whichever version of them is singled out, and by the political trajectory that this has in any one instance.

That such exclusions are constitutive of discourse is one of the central tenets of deconstruction in my understanding – including forms of deconstruction which, as in some of Spivak's early work, are rerouted in the direction of social theory and, as such, of ontology. Social theory cannot avoid producing ontologies, whether explicitly or implicitly, given that any assertion concerning 'society' or 'history' makes for an ontological claim; that is, for a claim that ontolog*izes* as given or 'real' the discursive objects with reference to which it makes its assertions. Practicing social theory and analysis with a deconstructive edge in my view means, first and foremost, attending to the exclusions which are entailed in assertions as to 'fact' or 'truth', whether such assertions feature as part of scholarly work or in other kinds of practice. Deconstruction in the sort of textual analyses of social relations which Spivak has produced from early on in her career, with a focus upon social relations as configured and enacted in other scholarly work (e.g. 1988a; 1988b; 1988c), can serve as a critical corrective and counterpart, then, to other kinds of political practice, including the production of social analysis and theory of more materialist kinds. In line with this view, Spivak has stated:

"[T]he irreducible but impossible task is to preserve the discontinuities within the discourses of feminism, Marxism and deconstruction. [...] If I have learned anything it is that one must not go in the direction of a Unification Church, which is too deeply marked by the colonialist influence, creating global solutions that are coherent. On the other hand, it seems to me that one must also avoid as much as possible, in the interests of practical effectiveness, a sort of continuist definition of the differences, so that all you get is hostility" (1990, 15).

In the interview from which this quotation is taken, Spivak proceeds to give examples of what she means by this, stemming from divergent locations in the theoretical spectrum of left-wing politics of the 1980s, when this interview was held: "[T]he slogan 'Marxist is sexist' bears this hostility, not understanding that it is a method that is used in very different ways" (1990, 15). As another example of a "continuist definition of the differences" between various theories, she parodies the critique according to which "[o]f course deconstruction [...] is only textualist, it is only esoteric, concerned with self-aggrandizement, nihilist, etc." (1990, 15). And Spivak concludes her overall observation by stating: "To preserve these discontinuities [...] rather than either wanting to look for an elegant coherence or producing a continuist discourse which will then result in hostility. I think that is what I want to do" (1990, 15).

Rather than either play competing approaches against each other, deciding that one must be entirely superior, on the one hand *or*, on the other, seeking to reconcile them in an overarching perspective, Spivak, in accordance with this statement, advocates deploying different theories in such as way that they bring each other to productive crisis (1990, 110–111). That is certainly what she may be said to be doing with a view to Marxism as a primarily ontological perspective and deconstruction as a primarily epistemological one (e.g. Spivak 1988a, esp. 280).

I want to address two cases in point as to what I consider to be unproductive about seeking either entirely to reconcile ontologically and epistemologically accentuated theoretical perspectives or playing them against each other as mutually exclusive, as Hemmings charges has recently occurred in Cultural Studies. I wish to do so in order to concretize what is at stake in this discussion. Negri and Hardt, too, have polarized both scholarly projects against each other, declaring deconstruction *passé*:

> "[T]he deconstructive phase of critical thought, which from Heidegger and Adorno to Derrida provided a powerful instrument for the exit from modernity, has lost its effectiveness. It is now a closed parenthesis and leaves us faced with a new task: constructing, in the non-place, a new place; constructing ontologically new determinations of the human, of living – a powerful artificiality of being. Donna Haraway's cyborg fable, which resides at the ambiguous boundary between human, animal, and machine, introduces us today, much more effectively than deconstruction, to these new terrains of possibility" (2001, 217–218).

In line with the analysis I presented earlier, I view Negri's and Hardt's dismissal of deconstruction as historically obsolete, and their one-sided commitment to constructing new ontologies in its stead, as being related to what previously I had argued forms a rather un-self-conscious celebration of 'minor' subjects on their part – whose resistance they declare to be substantively autonomous (Hardt/Negri 2001, e.g. xv, 43, 124) in much the way Deleuze, in one of the quotations given earlier, celebrates those who speak on their own behalf as inherently revolutionary in outlook. As I have argued, deconstruction focuses the critic's attention upon the textual and, hence, the 'arbitrary', fictional dimension of all practice and sharpens our awareness of what exclusions are entailed in any one discursive move. Ideally, this should foster self-consciousness on the analyst's part as to the dimensions of power entailed in the relations of representation in which she is herself implicated in virtue of writing and publishing. In contrast, Hardt and Negri would seem to be *ontologizing* the analysis they present of 'Empire' and 'the multitude' wholeheartedly, treating it as *the* one way of conceiving of our global present. This is to cover over, rather than to cultivate awareness of, the critic's own positionality and politics, and hence, of her own implication in the power relations she analyzes *or* potentially excludes from analysis.

But – to develop Spivak's argument with a view to the relationship between epistemology and ontology – to seek to reconcile both perspectives as if this entailed no loss, as if they were wholeheartedly commensurable is equally unadvisable in my view. I want briefly to address Barad's rather different brand of post-Deleuzian theorizing as a case in point – rather different, that is, from Hardt's and Negri's development of the thought of Deleuze. Barad presents her approach of agential realism (a variant of new materialism) as an *"[o]nto-epistem-ology"* or *"ethico-onto-epistem-ology"* (2007, 185; emphasis in the original; see also Barad 2007, 25–26). According to her posthumanist philosophy, since there is nothing fundamental to distinguish humanity either from other animate life or from inanimate matter, there is no need to differentiate human knowledge from other forms of knowing (Barad 2007, 323, 331–332, 338, 341–342, 419, n. 27, 177–178, 437, n. 81) (see chapter 1 of this book). It is sufficient in her view to circumscribe knowledge by the formula – repeated time and again in her book, *Meeting the Universe Halfway* – that "part of the world [makes] itself intelligible to another part" (Barad 2007, 185; see also Barad 2007, 176, 140, 342, 379). It does not matter in Barad's view whether the 'subjects' and 'objects', which in such processes are only situationally differentiated into these respective parts, are humans or brittlestars intra-acting (to use her neologism) with and as part of their ocean environment (see Barad 2007, 378–380). While Barad claims that her theory incorporates epistemology, she offers no particular account as to *what* epistemological perspective – what theory of knowledge in particular – her philosophy entails. This is in line with the fact that the latter admits of no fundamental difference between human, animate and inanimate 'matter': Epistemology is effectively replaced by an *"ontology* of knowing" (Barad 2007, 378; emphasis added; see also Barad 2007, 379) – or, more appropriately phrased in my view, of communication – in which divergent *perspectives, subjectivities* and *experiences* have no part to play. Thus Barad's account seems not to permit consideration of the 'perspectival' character of knowledge, of the different *sides* which there are to any one 'story'. As a result, the power relations entailed in the social production, discursive arrangement, and unequal dissemination of *competing* knowledges would seem to be difficult to analyze within the framework of Barad's approach. This is particularly problematic considering that her theorizing is, of course, *an instance* of knowledge production, yielding effects of power of its own, qua major intellectual trend.[1] Thus its partial, 'arbitrary' or contingent, and necessarily exclusionary character qua *specific discursive perspective* remains unmarked as such, and unreflected, in Barad's writing. The following statement by her seems to me to invoke a world that literally *desires* to be known or discovered – a displacement, in my reading, of *the author-subject's desire* for discovery which thus remains unacknowledged, and which I find to resonate uncomfortably with colonial discourses:

> "If we no longer believe that the world is teeming with inherent resemblances whose signatures are inscribed on the face of the world, things already emblazoned with signs, words lying in wait like so many pebbles of sand on a beach *there to be discovered*, but rather that the knowing subject is enmeshed in a thick web of representations such that the mind cannot see its way to objects that are now forever out of reach and all that is visible is the sticky problem of humanity's own captivity within language, then it becomes apparent that representationalism is a prisoner of the problematic metaphysics it postulates" (Barad 2007, 137; emphasis added).

In Barad's theoretical account, then, much as it purports to reconcile epistemology and ontology, her attempt to build a 'Unification Church'

---

1   To concretize, one such effect of power is that agential realism ultimately tends to render invisible social *differentials* of power, understood in terms of highly divergent degrees to which differently situated subjects, collective as well as individual, succeed or fail to succeed in *making* their knowledges, and actions, 'matter' or 'materialize' as (politically transformed) reality. Put differently, Barad's generalizing assertion of the power of matter covers over the relative powerlessness of the socially excluded and marginalized.

– to use Spivak's expression (see above) – implicitly privileges ontology at the expense of epistemology: anything that may be particular to a human, discursively constituted form of knowledge is subsumed (flattened out, I am tempted to say, echoing Hemmings) under theoretical phrasings that operate at an extremely high level of generality as a direct result of the fact that posthumanism – at least in Barad's version of it – flattens out differences between human and non-human subjects as well as between animate and inanimate matter. Let us remember that Spivak has characterized theoretical moves "in the direction of a Unification Church" such that they are "too deeply marked by the colonialist influence, creating global solutions that are coherent" (see above). This characterization would seem to allude to the identitarian, totalizing thrust of producing a theoretical account that purports to *include everything*. Since, at least according to deconstruction, it is impossible to do so, the effect will be (as argued by Spivak) "colonialist" in trajectory: some elements will be privileged at the expense of others without the resulting unevenness being marked as such.

The privilege which ontology is implicitly assigned vis-à-vis epistemology in Barad's proposal for fusing the two parallels Negri's and Hardt's explicit favoring of ontology over and against the supposedly outdated concerns of deconstruction:[2] In these two

---

2   It would seem to follow from Hardt's and Negri's commitment to posthumanism, as formulated in the following quotations, that even epistemology, more generally – qua theory of human, discursively constituted knowledge – is not considered by them to form an essential dimension of critical practice:

"There is a strict continuity between the religious thought that accords a power above nature to God and the modern 'secular' thought that accords the same power above nature to Man. The transcendence of God is simply transferred to Man. Like God before it, this Man that stands separate from and above nature has no place in a philosophy of immanence. Like God, too, this transcendent figure of Man leads quickly to the imposition of social hierarchy and domination" (Hardt/Negri 2001, 91).

"[H]uman nature is in no way separate from nature as a whole, [...] there are no fixed and necessary boundaries between the human and the animal, the

instances at least, whether the two perspectives are played against each other or are supposedly reconciled, one of them – specifically: a focus on the politics of knowledge – tends to be subordinated, if not occluded. In scholarly work which partakes in what might be termed the knowledge industry – a significant force in hegemonic struggle – this has a depoliticizing effect. Namely, in that progressively intended contributions to this struggle tend not to be reflexive about their own effects of power; including the relations which they set up between the representing subject (as an author as well as institutionally speaking) and what or who is being represented.

Any attempt to invert the discursive arrangements described above, such that *epistemology* will be privileged one-sidedly over and against *ontology* – as it often was during the early, twentieth-century phase of poststructuralist writing – would obviously be no more satisfactory. To seek to limit questions of power to epistemological concerns and thus, to the politics of *knowledge*, in particular, would be to erase from view the economic, political, and social dimensions of relations of domination to the extent that these exceed the purely discursive – a point to which I shall return at the end of this chapter.

Towards a third alternative

How, then, *are* we to envision the relationship between epistemological and ontological dimensions of analyzing, and critiquing, power relations in less reductive ways? It seems to me that it is impossible to do equal justice at the same time to epistemological and ontological concerns. For, on the one hand, in order to focus upon the textual level of how any given object of discourse is constituted so as to examine how its 'reality effect' (Barthes 2006b) is generated, we must necessarily bracket our own sense of reality and strive to suspend any truth claims we would otherwise be making. When, on the other hand, we place

---

human and the machine, the male and the female, and so forth" (Hardt/Negri 2001, 215).

our focus upon the ontological features of a given object of inquiry, we inevitably throw in our lot *with a given version* of what is 'the case'. Both perspectives are, as I see it, incommensurable.

We should therefore abstain from declaring any single theoretical perspective superior; a move which would arrogate something akin to omniscience to that perspective. Since no one theory can avoid producing exclusions that will underwrite the particularity, and the political merits, of the perspective which it establishes, no one theory can justifiably make a claim to being autonomous and wholly adequate or politically satisfactory in the 'take' upon power relations which it offers. All theorizing then – Spivakean deconstruction as much as ontologies such as those produced by Barad and by Negri/Hardt, respectively – in principle is in need of being supplemented by alternative, complementary perspectives.

For the above reasons, it seems necessary to me in any one research effort to prioritize self-consciously: Do the questions and the theoretical perspective in terms of which it is framed accentuate primarily epistemological or ontological concerns? Whichever dimensions of power relations are *not* in focus should, all the same, be de-prioritized consciously, without being ignored entirely. Working epistemological and ontological features of social research and cultural analysis against each other such that they might bring one another 'to productive crisis' could mean producing, on the one hand, ontologies that strive for maximal reflexivity with a view to their own discursive character, about the contingencies entailed in any one manner of constituting 'reality', and about the inescapable exclusions attendant upon doing so. Vigilance as to one's own role as part of the power-implicative and always situated institutional production of knowledge should help forestall rhetorics such as the un-self-conscious one Spivak has criticized in Deleuze and Foucault on the specific occasion of their conversation, as much as a colonizing rhetoric such as I have problematized in Barad along with Negri and Hardt. For instance, if Negri and Hardt didn't dismiss deconstruction as historically obsolete quite so readily, they might be more cognizant of discursive critiques of exoticism – modern and postmodern – such as the one formulated by hooks, as discussed above, in which I have argued they themselves engage.

When pursuing scholarly research that is primarily epistemologically focused, on the other hand, we need to keep in mind the fact that (as argued earlier) social inquiry in the widest sense, even when it proceeds by deconstructive methodologies or poststructuralist discourse analysis, cannot steer clear entirely of being complicit with ontologizing gestures and statements of 'fact'. "[O]ne cannot not be an essentialist", as Spivak too has argued (1990, 45). As she elaborates, deconstruction is "an examination, over and over again, of the fact that we are obliged to produce truths, positive things" (1990, 46). "That's the thing that deconstruction gives us; an awareness that what we are obliged to do, and must do scrupulously, in the long run is not OK" (Spivak 1990, 45). In other words, since we cannot wholly abstain from making truth claims as to 'empirical reality' or 'facts' – at least as part of producing social research, as I would add – it is all the more necessary to be cognizant of the ontologizing character of such claims. As a poststructuralist, epistemologically sensitive analytic methodology, deconstruction is helpful in reminding us that we need to mark at the metalevel the fact that all ontology is ultimately more appropriately referred to as *ontologization*.

Strictly speaking, moreover, even an *epistemological* perspective as such is capable of being ontologized as a matter of truth devoid of discursive mediation: If, by 'epistemology', we understand (as I have done in this chapter) a metaperspective upon discourses which brackets the question as to whether their objects are 'real', so as to bring into view discourses' constitutive exclusions and the effects of power generated in virtue of such exclusion, it is certainly possible – yet problematic, too – to render absolute this metaperspective, naturalizing it in turn by losing sight of its 'perspectival' character. That would mean, in turn, naturalizing *this* particular perspective (the 'discursive' perspective), its constitutive exclusions, and hence, its effects of power. If, by 'ontology', we understand (as I have done in this chapter) a perspective which takes as given or 'real' the objects of its own discourse, then it is possible and, indeed, seems necessary to me to conceive of ontology and epistemology as *each others'* respective constitutive outsides. As such, each of these perspectives is necessary as a critique of the reductions or 'biases' entailed in (that is, a critique of the partial character of) the other one, and only when their character as competing perspectives is kept in mind can their respective effects of power come into view. For instance, 'class' as understood in Marxist theory can be treated, alternatively, as a given of social reality to be analyzed for its *material* effects of power *or* as an object of discourse, the specific construction of which produces *discursive* effects of power – e.g. when 'class' is analytically privileged over and against race and gender as a constituent of social relations of domination. A rigorous critique of relations of domination in their different dimensions makes it necessary to refrain from 'opting' for either an epistemological or an ontological perspective to the exclusion of its counterpart as a matter of principle. For, to stay with my example, it would be as problematic to ontologize a Marxist frame for understanding social relations as self-sufficient (i.e. not in need, for instance, of the supplement of an intersectional analysis of social inequality) as it would be to treat a (deconstructive-) discursive perspective as self-sufficient. For, in the latter case, power would be reduced to its discursive dimensions to the detriment of its material (e.g. economic) aspects.

It is because *all* discourses necessarily produce exclusions – rendering invisible features of 'reality' that are perceivable only from an *alternative* perspective – that deconstructive analysis in Spivak's hands has meant shuttling between alternative perspectives. However, much as the theoretico-political need for an awareness of the specificity of any one perspective makes it necessary to *distinguish* such perspectives – as I have argued with a view to the difference between epistemology and ontology – bringing to bear deconstructive analysis and critique upon social relations means that neither 'epistemology' nor 'ontology' can be practiced 'purely', without becoming entangled in a complicity of sorts with its respective counterpart. (Which is not to say that the two perspectives are commensurable, let alone 'essentially the same'.) For, after all, such practice asserts the fictional status of any given discursive construction or positivity as much as its 'real' effects of power. To the extent that this is the case, deconstructive social analysis will to some degree oscillate between making epistemological *and* making ontological claims, and will always be at risk of essentializing (naturalizing) *both*. We should be worried less about the contradictory character of doing so, and more about the very tendency to essentialize either perspective. Inescapable as it may be to do so – "one cannot not be an essentialist" (Spivak, as quoted above) – it is as a way of self-critically marking this tendency at the metalevel that deconstruction teaches us to be vigilant.

I would like to clarify what is at stake here by reference to Dennis Bruining's recent treatment (2016) of the debate on new materialism (see also chapter 1 of this book). In particular, I wish to exemplify, based on his article, the fact that discourse theory – much as it takes an epistemological perspective, as such – is not immune to ontologizing *itself*. It therefore is not immune to falling into the trap which above I have argued is entailed in privileging ontology over and against epistemology (whether explicitly, as in Hardt's and Negri's work, or implicitly, as in Barad's): the trap of failing to reflect the discursive (constitutive or performative) status of one's own theoretical intervention, and hence, the fact that one thereby inescapably effects constitutive exclusions, since there can be no discourse without a constitutive outside (Butler 2003, 131; 1993, 3, 8, 22).

Bruining agrees with Sara Ahmed (2008) that the criticism, articulated by some new materialists, to the effect that poststrucuralists seek to proscribe engagement with 'material' dimensions of the world, mistakenly posits that poststructuralists 'reduce everything to language or discourse'. Bruining rightly points out that some writers identified with new materialism in turn operate with a notion of materiality that posits 'matter', including the human body, to be knowable *as if such knowledge were extricable from discourse*. As Bruining notes (in line with Ahmed's earlier argument), this view reinscribes the very dualism between discourse and materiality, or mind and matter (see chapter 1), that new materialism seeks to move beyond, and which some of its proponents charge *poststructuralists* with maintaining.

However, where (as argued above) Barad purports to fuse epistemology and ontology as if the two could be fully reconciled without any attendant loss or exclusion, to the effect of privileging ontology over and against epistemology (albeit implicitly rather than explicitly), I would argue that Bruining makes an analogous move, only with a bias of the opposite kind: In his account, *the discursive perspective* is treated as if adopting it did not *in turn produce constitutive exclusions*, i.e. as if it were no perspective at all but rather, simply 'the truth' in an unmediated sense. Ontological perspectives upon matter are constructed by Bruining as theoretically mistaken and illegitimate to the extent that they conflict with the former (discursive) perspective. This is, likewise, depoliticizing in that it is to naturalize the discursive, epistemological point of view in virtue of foreclosing alternative perspectives incommensurable with it. It is, in other words, *to ontologize the epistemological perspective.*

To an extent, it is surprising that Bruining should do so. For, in his article he defends a performative (in particular, a Butlerian) view of discourse, according to which to seek to *know* is performatively to affect – to reconstitute or reshape *in its ontology* – what is known. By way of this understanding of the relationship between the epistemic and the ontic, of knowing and being, Bruining articulates what I have been calling 'epistemology' and 'ontology' with each other as strongly interrelated. However, not entirely unlike Barad (albeit in the way of an inverted mirror image of her position), he so closely identifies the two with each other that the tension between them comes to be suppressed. In Bruining's version of the relationship between knowing and being, or what I refer to as the epistemological and the ontological, performativity or the constitution of what *is* by what is *known* is rendered as absolute, leaving no remainder. Thus, commenting upon a text by Samantha Frost (2014), he writes: "Frost posits the existence of things she calls hormonal and steroidal floods, nervous-system adjustments, and so on, instead of seeing them as performative effects. If Butler applied this same logic, this would mean positing selves before their performance, which, of course, she does not." (Bruining 2016, 33)

By *reducing* biological processes to performative effects as if they could be wholly analogized with purely discursive phenomena such as the notion of a 'self', Bruining subsumes what *is* under what is *known*, thereby subordinating ontology to epistemology in a move that is the inverse of the privilege which Barad as well as Negri and Hardt assign ontology vis-à-vis epistemology. While such subsumption as operated by Bruining is convincing in the case of phenomena which are exhaustively discursive in the sense that they would not exist in the absence of being discursively posited and constructed – such as the phenomenon of a 'self' – to treat biological processes as analogously purely performative (and hence, discursive) effects is to abnegate material processes that take shape *whether or not they are known* (and hence reconstituted, i.e. shaped) as part of human, discursive practices.

In turn, this means rendering the discursive perspective as 'true, unmediated knowledge', thereby failing to apply the notion of performativity at the metalevel, i.e. to one's own discourse. If Bruining were to treat the theoretical (Butlerian, discursive-performative) stance which he defends as *itself* performative, he would have to relativize it as a *specific perspective producing effects of power*, partially in virtue of the constitutive exclusions it is premised upon and enabled by. Instead, Bruining only heeds the exclusionary, power-charged character *of perspectives that engage in ontological speculation* about the shape of what *is* to the extent that 'what is' is not reducible to what we *know*, and how we know it. He thereby undertakes a move of reducing all there is to be 'legitimately' explored in theoretical terms to an examination of the world *as we know it*. I perceive this as, indeed, amounting to a proscribing gesture (of the kind some new materialists have argued is engaged in by poststructuralists [see Ahmed 2008; Bruining 2016]) that styles the perspective from which it proceeds as existing outside power. Were Bruining to grant the discursive status of the theoretical perspective from which his own argument proceeds, he could not dismiss ontological speculation (as to 'being' beyond 'knowing') as theoretically mistaken, *as if the discursive (epistemological) perspective which he adopts were devoid of exclusionary, power-charged foreclosures*.

While Bruining's article discusses only new materialist work that takes an interest in *bodily* materiality, one constitutive outside to his discussion consists in the material – that is to say, the more-than-purely-discursive – dimensions of power as a more encompassing *social* phenomenon. As argued further above, unegalitarian effects of power can be most fully critiqued when a number of complementary perspectives on its operations are adopted. Power is not exhausted by its discursive aspects. Environmental racism (Tuana 2008) would be one example of how social inequality and the biopolitical abjection of certain subjects' lives are impacted by factors not *reducible* to discourses. *Pace* Bruining, such impact – for instance, the manufacture of plastic and the increased incidence of cancer among workers in this industry, which radically reduces some subjects' life span (Tuana 2008) – may take shape even *when no human subject is aware of it.* The fact that saying so is already a discursive statement, and that there can be no knowledge of this causal link that would not already be discursive, does not obviate the political importance of research that proceeds *as if* such links could be known in 'non-discursive' ways – that is, as if producing knowledge about this subject did not in turn affect the matter under investigation performatively at an ontological level.

Precisely if knowledge is not treated purely as an end in itself but, instead, as political and oriented to the goal of contributing to the achievement of more egalitarian social relations, we cannot afford to declare any one theoretical perspective self-sufficient. Since critiquing social relations of domination and effects of power requires in part the adoption of ontologizing perspectives that proceed in such an 'as if' mode as just described, and hence with a certain theoretical naïvety, it is not only legitimate but politically necessary to leave behind a stance that privileges a discursive, epistemologically accentuated perspective as somehow superior and fully 'right'. The latter stance would amount to a thoroughly un-performative view of one's own discursive practice, which would itself exhibit theoretical naïvety precisely in virtue of disavowing *its own (exclusionary) effects of power.* If Bruining ends his article by invoking Jacques Derrida's statement "that 'whoever believes that one tracks down some *thing;* one tracks down tracks'" (Bruining

2016, 37, citing Derrida; emphasis in the original) and reminds us that "despite the fact that we may expect matter, nature and/or substance to precede its trace, we can only ever find its trace" (Bruining 2016, 37), I would encourage us to become theoretically less 'purist', in scrupulous complicity with alternative, *mutually complementary* forms of naïvety – based upon the realization that we cannot refrain entirely from such theoretical naïvety or reductiveness. (A realization that should come with the poststructuralist conviction that, to paraphrase Butler [2003, 131; 1993, 3, 8, 22], there is no discourse without a constitutive outside.) Let us "[track] down tracks" with full awareness of the fact that tracks or traces is what we are dealing with when we engage in ontological speculation, in theoretically impure speculation about what there is 'beyond' – not reducible to – discourse. It is impossible to engage in discursive practices without being reductive in one way or the other. It is in this spirit that I shall proceed in the chapters that follow.

3 Affect/Discourse
A Chiastic Relationship
On Judith Butler, Margaret Wetherell, and the Affective Turn

Introduction: Why theorize feeling?[1]

A turn to affect has been highly necessary for poststructuralist theory and Cultural Studies. Until the beginnings of the affective turn, the notion of 'discourse', as deployed by Michel Foucault and others, tended to be used in a way that isolated it from emotions, that is, in a rationalist and – thus – a reductive form (see, e.g., Foucault 1972; Macdonnell 1986; Fairclough 1989; Wetherell/Potter 1992). In effect, if not in intention, the widespread theoretical isolation of discourses from emotions reinscribed the hierarchical opposition between reason and emotion which has been central among the set of hierarchical oppositions constitutive of what, during the 1990s, was referred to as modern or 'Enlightenment' discourse (see, e.g., Hulme/Jordanova 1990; Gilroy 1993). In fact, the opposition 'discourse/affect', which forms a poststructuralist variant of the opposition 'reason/emotion', tended to be neglected in feminist, postcolonial and other critical scholarly projects which otherwise aimed to deconstruct hierarchical oppositions that are implicated in gendered, racialized and other inequalities (see,

---

1   As explained further below in the main text, I use the terms 'feeling', 'affect' and 'emotion' synonymously, contrary to recent convention.

e.g., Spivak 1988a, 1990; Bhabha 1994). The turn to affect has been a
necessary consequence drawn from the latent rationalism of earlier
poststructuralisms, as entailed in their cognitive reductionism.

Without a focus on emotions, the call – and the desire – for political
change is in fact less than fully intelligible: If social inequality, and
the discursive hierarchies which serve to sustain it, did not tend to
produce suffering or some sort of emotional discomfort, then why
should anyone bother to seek political change? This question clarifies
why politicized scholarly inquiry into 'discourse' makes it necessary
to theorize feeling at the same time: Early theorizations of discourse
influenced by poststructuralism, for all their critical impetus, were
unable to provide an answer to it. They lacked a theoretical vocabulary
for addressing the *emotional costs* of unegalitarian discourses and modes
of social organization.[2]

But has the affective turn moved us beyond the dualism of discourse
vs. feeling? Has it fully taken account of what I construe as the major
reason why a turn to affect has been necessary for poststructuralism –
namely, the need to move beyond that dualism? In this chapter, I argue
that some of the main trends in theorizing feeling have, on the contrary,
reproduced this dualism – in forms that remain hierarchizing and,
thus, continue to be complicit with unegalitarian politics. This applies
equally to rationalist, cognitively reductionist notions of emotion,

---

2   I adapt the notion that subordination and exclusion are emotionally costly
to those negatively affected thereby from Arlie Russell Hochschild's similar
argument, according to which *emotional labor*, as demanded by corporations
from their workforce (such as the flight attendants whose labor conditions and
emotional strategies she examined), generates "human costs" or "psychological
costs", as she puts it (2003, 186–187). Whereas Hochschild's analysis of these
costs relies upon the problematic, essentialist notion of "estrangement" (2003,
37), I am suggesting that social subordination and exclusion are *emotionally*
costly in that they tend to generate suffering or at least some sense of affective
discomfort. See also note 15 to this chapter.
Heather Love similarly emphasizes the costs of social exclusion and denigration
in a way which seems to link to her emphasis on "feelings such as grief, regret,
and despair" (2007b, 163).

which tend to reduce the latter to their discursive dimension (e.g. Nussbaum 2001; Reddy 2001; Illouz 2008; Wetherell 2012, 2015; McAvoy 2015; Leys 2017) – thus subordinating emotion to discourse – *and* to notions of affect which, on the contrary, celebrate affect as the Other of discourse, whilst privileging it vis-à-vis the latter category (e.g. Thrift 2008; Massumi 2002). I argue that a feminist, antiracist and, generally, egalitarian politics of emotion needs to move beyond this impasse rather than positioning itself *within* either theoretical camp (see also Fischer 2016).

This chapter makes one proposal for how to conceive of the relationship between feeling and discourse in non-hierarchizing fashion, namely, in terms of the rhetorical figure of the chiasm (a crossing). This figure has been invoked repeatedly by Judith Butler – even though she barely discusses its significance explicitly – in ways that begin to move beyond dualism (understood as an absolutist, non-relational rendering of difference) and beyond identitarian thinking (understood as an assimilationist erasure of difference) at once. For instance, Butler has theorized the relationship between discourse or language and the body, between passivity and activity, and (drawing upon Maurice Merleau-Ponty's philosophy) between subject and object as well as feeling and knowing as chiastic; as involving constitutive ties or transitions between the terms making up each of these conceptual pairs, yet without identifying the respective oppositional terms with each other (Butler 2015a, 178–180; 2015b, 14–22, 41–62, 155–170). The figure of the chiasm has much affinity with the feminist notion of intersectionality, but I consider it to be a potentially useful model for thinking difference and relationality together, more generally.

Unlike Butler, however, I will highlight the potential for tension entailed in the figure of the chiasm, more than a blurring of contrary terms into each other, as she tends to do. I do so in the interest of moving beyond hierarchical thinking, to which Butler's theorization of the relationship between feeling and knowing remains indebted in my view (2015b, 41–62; see also Butler 2015b, 155–170). (I would argue that her analysis here risks an identitarian assimilation of thinking to feeling, which privileges the second term as primary [compare note 5 to this chapter].) I thus wish respectfully to tap the potential for non-hierarchizing thinking which I view as being entailed in the notion of a chiasm, as elucidated by Butler at other points in her work (Butler 2015a, 120–121, 178–180; 2015b, 14–22). In drawing upon these, and further, productive moments of her theorizing as a way of framing the relationship between emotions and discourse – and how power bears upon it – I hope to begin to emulate "double-edged thinking" (Butler 2004b, 129), as commendably practiced by Butler herself in many parts of her writing. This account supplements and modifies my earlier attempt to think emotions along Butlerian lines (Braunmühl 2012b).

In what follows, I begin by critiquing the reductive tendencies in existing research on emotions which I have problematized above. Then I outline what it might mean to conceptualize the relationship between discourse and affect as chiastic. Next, I discuss how power might most fruitfully be understood in relation to these terms, so as to arrive at a politicized, critical, theoretically grounded account of discourse and its relationship to emotions. I make this proposal by way of contrast with Margaret Wetherell's account of affective-discursive practice (2015; 2012) – which, as I argue, subordinates affect to discourse whilst deploying a notion of discourse that is insufficiently critical. In concluding, I briefly consider from a feminist perspective the political implications of the alternative proposal made in this chapter, in both theoretical and practical terms.

Two opposing, but equally reductive, trends in recent theorizations of feeling

Affect theory has been critiqued widely for opposing affect to emotion in a manner that ultimately replicates the dualism of body vs. mind (Leys 2017; Wetherell 2015; McAvoy 2015; Barnett 2008), as associated with categories such as 'discourse' and 'the social'. Thus Clare Hemmings has written, commenting upon the work of Brian Massumi (2002) and Eve Kosofsky Sedgwick (2003):

"My critical response to Massumi and Sedgwick's work on affect, then, is not one that rejects the importance of affect for cultural theory. It is one that rejects the contemporary fascination with affect as outside social meaning, as providing a break in both the social and in critics' engagements with the nature of the social. The problems in Massumi and Sedgwick discussed in this article do not require a wholesale rejection of affect's relevance to cultural theory. Instead, affect might in fact be valuable precisely to the extent that it is not autonomous" (Hemmings 2005, 564–565).

As Clive Barnett asserts with reference to Nigel Thrift's 'non-representational theory' and other post-foundational approaches which proceed "in terms of 'layer-cake' ontologies of practice" – where "[a]ffect is presented as an ontological layer of embodied existence" that is "layered below the level of minded, intentional consciousness" (2008, 188): "there is a tendency to simply assert the conceptual priority of previously denigrated terms – affect over reason, practice over representation" (Barnett 2008, 188). The problem, then, is that in the work of writers such as Massumi and Thrift, affect remains the Other of discourse and is conceived of in terms of a normative hierarchy – albeit one inverted relative to modern convention, with affect at the top and reason or discourse positioned as its maligned antagonist. For instance, Thrift writes in *Non-Representational Theory* that much of the interest in the role of affect in politics manifested in the existing literature, including feminist literature, on politics "has been bedevilled by the view that politics ought to be about conscious, rational discourse with the result that affect is regarded as at best an add-on and as at worst a dangerous distraction" (2008, 248). But Thrift in *Non-Representational Theory* inverts the very normative arrangement which he imputes to such work into its plain opposite, into a mere mirror image of what he is critiquing: He frames politics as being essentially about 'affect', with 'conscious, rational discourse' relegated to the role of mere add-on. What is missing here is any sense of how affect and discourse might *complicate one another*; any *relational* account of these terms.

However, rather than moving beyond this dissatisfactory state of affairs towards a truly relational account of discourse and feeling, some of those who critique affect theory in these terms tend, for their part, to invert the above trend in a way that over-identifies emotions with discourse, subordinating the former to the latter by reducing feelings to their discursive dimension.[3] They thereby continue the modern or 'Enlightenment' convention of subordinating emotions to reason or discourse, that is, to cognition – albeit in a variant which renders emotions as a *dimension* of cognition rather than as its Other. In what is perhaps the most extreme example of this tendency, which must be characterized as identitarian, Ruth Leys asserts – presumably, but not explicitly with reference to the *psychological* research of affect, in particular – that "in the field of emotion research there is no intellectually viable alternative to [Alan J.] Fridlund's position" (2017, 368).[4] This position, according to Leys, holds "that emotions are conceptual through and through" (2017, 275). In fact, Fridlund is agnostic on the question of *whether there are emotions* at all (Leys 2017, 361–362, 275–276). Accordingly, his research does not concern itself with emotions (2017, 358–368), but instead studies "intentional actions of intact animals" (2017, 363) (including human animals) as inferred from their observable interactions. Leys' endorsement of Fridlund's position therefore seems to amount to endorsing such research as a satisfactory alternative capable of *replacing*, if not the academic study of affect *tout court*, then at least its psychological investigation. It would hardly seem possible to subordinate (by way of assimilating) emotion to cognition

---

3   An exception to this is J. S. Hutta's contribution to the debate, in which the author states: "Affect, then, not only drives discourse, but discourse also conditions affect" (Hutta 2015, 298). Interestingly, this perspective of both shaping each other *mutually* coincides, in Hutta's article – as it does in this text – with an emphasis on dynamism in the relationship between semiotics or discourse and affect (2015, 304). As I suggest in the main text, this emphasis is allowed for by conceiving of that relationship in *non-hierarchizing* terms.

4   My remarks here pertain solely to how Leys reconstructs Fridlund's position and are intended as a criticism of Leys' text rather than of Fridlund's research itself – which I have not studied independently of its representation by Leys.

in terms more absolute than these, which amount, literally, to *dissolving* the former into the latter.[5]

Martha Nussbaum similarly reduces emotions to value-laden cognitions or "judgments of value" (2001, 19); a position she herself refers to as a "'cognitive-evaluative' view" (2001, 23).[6] William M. Reddy defines emotion in terms of "[t]he constant activation of *thought material* associated with the complex tasks of goal coordination" (2001, 121; emphasis added), where "all such loosely aggregated thought activations [are] considered 'emotions'" (2001, 94; see also Reddy 2001, 321; 2008, 80–81, n. 1). And in my final example of the stated trend in research on emotion – of an identitarian reduction of feeling to its discursive or cognitive dimension – Wetherell (2015; 2012) defines affect in terms of practices which accompany any and all *discursive* practice. By reducing affect to a practice and an accompaniment of discourse, she, too, produces an account which misses the sense in which emotions can

---

5   See also the critique of Leys (2011) offered by John Cromby and Martin E. H. Willis (2016, 483). These authors, however, in turn invert the hierarchy in favor of cognition which they rightly critique in Leys' work. They do so in virtue of presenting an account of the relationship between 'feeling' and cognition according to which (in line with the philosophies of Alfred North Whitehead and Susanne Langer) 'feeling' is privileged as primary. Their account thus presents the case of an *identitarian* theory of said relationship which tends to assimilate, and to subordinate, discourse to feeling (see esp. 2016, 486) – which in turn is conceptualized in terms that privilege body over mind. This chapter, by contrast, aims to provide a *non-hierarchizing*, even-handed account of the relationship between feeling and discourse. I suggest that in order to move beyond hierarchical thinking, we need to problematize not only dualism but also identitarian, assimilatory versions of such thinking (which, in the case of theorizing the relationship between emotion and discourse, fail to provide for the possibility of tension between these). Cromby and Willis only problematize dualistic versions of such thinking. In line with this, they critique Leys' account as dualistic rather than as identitarian, as I do.

6   Nussbaum (2001) also hypostatizes the intelligibility of emotions to a degree which renders the human subject as potentially fully self-transparent. This rationalist view is incompatible with any notion of the unconscious as irreducible, which informs the theoretical account to be presented in what follows.

disrupt discourses and exceed their logic; the sense in which emotions can even work against the logic of already-constituted discourses, potentially contributing to their transformation. (I will return to this lacuna, and others, in her account further below.)

As long as the study of feelings is shaped by a dichotomy, whereby feeling is *either* over-*identified* with discourse or cognition in a way that ultimately renders it as a quasi-discursive activity *or* is – alternatively – *dissociated* from discourse, we remain faithful in one way or another to variants of the hierarchical opposition of reason or discourse vs. emotion bequeathed to us by modern convention. We do so, *both* when we celebrate affect as the (now-preferred) Other of discourse, *and* when we subordinate it to discourse by reducing it to a dimension of the latter.

The dualistic, hierarchical arrangement of modern discourses has been critiqued extensively for being implicated in gendered, racialized, and further inequalities constitutive of modernity (see chapter 1). The discourse/affect opposition is an indisputable case in point, given how it has served – and continues to serve – to render women, People of Color, and other marginalized or excluded subjects as irrational and, as such, as lesser forms of life. This is why a feminist, intersectional, egalitarian politics cannot rest content with theoretical accounts of feeling which position the latter in a hierarchical relationship to discourse – no matter which of these terms is being privileged over the other: Any such hierarchy will remain gendered and racialized at least by association, and thus, forestalls any truly egalitarian conceptual move beyond hierarchies of race and gender. Due to the historically gendered and racialized dimension of hierarchical arrangements of the conceptual pair of reason/affectivity, in particular, any such arrangement which continues to construct affectivity as the Other of discourse risks reinscribing the connotation of affectivity with racialized and gendered Otherness and vice-versa, over and against 'reason' – even when the conventional hierarchy of 'reason over emotion' is turned on its head in what amounts to a mere reverse discourse. As for the inverse tendency in existing research on emotions to reduce the latter to their discursive dimension, the latent rationalism entailed in this reinscribes the masculinism of 'Enlightenment' thinking, effacing and thereby implicitly devaluing difference (i.e. what is irreducible about affect, including its nonrational, historically feminized as well as devalued dimension). A feminist, egalitarian politics committed to reducing social inequalities and exclusions – including their affective dimensions (Ahmed 2010; Love 2007b; Hemmings 2005, 561–562) – must therefore trouble both any identitarian *identification* of emotions with discourse which tends to assimilate the former to the latter, and any neat *separation* of both terms. It requires an account of emotion that does justice to *both* the intimate relatedness of these categories *and* the potential for tension between them – that is, to their irreducibility to one another. Only with such an account do we stand a chance of leaving behind the complicity of theory with gendered, racialized, and further inequalities. In order to commit to this goal, it will not do to either equate 'affectivity' with 'reason/rationality' or split these terms apart.

Much (queer-)feminist work on emotion has, in fact, refused either variety of reductionism (see, e.g., Ahmed 2010; Cvetkovich 2012; Love 2007b). However, the conceptualization of emotions which such work has offered is not always very clear with a view to *how*, exactly, to think the relationship between emotions and discourse. In what follows, I propose that the rhetorical figure of the chiasm has much potential for fleshing out how these categories can be conceptualized as being irreducible to each other, while at the same time being mutually implicated.

Discourse/feeling: a chiasm

Feelings according to the theoretical account proposed here are framed by discursive scripts which tend to limit, along with enabling, the spectrum of what can be felt at a given historical moment.[7] These

---

7   I have previously stated this tendency in terms too absolute (Braunmühl 2012b, 225), thus failing to allow for the notion, developed in this chapter, that "discourses must also be understood as themselves being potentially impinged

scripts – understood in terms of matrices of intelligibility that are formative of the human subject – are highly racialized, gendered and class-specific, assigning diverging norms of affective performance, experience, and mutual response to hierarchically differentiated social groups. Thus, for instance, Sara Ahmed (2014, 86–87) in her analysis of disgust touches, by reference to prior work by Audre Lorde (1984, 147–148), upon how persons of Color have come historically to be associated with 'offensiveness' and the affect of disgust in the racist experience of many 'whites' (see also Hemmings 2005, 561–562). Clearly, disgust – including disgust incited by racist discourses – has a strong bodily, visceral dimension, which thus cannot coherently be dichotomized against its discursive dimension. Similarly, 'white' fear of (young) Black men in the U.S. context is a case in point which illustrates the social, discursive character of even the most visceral dimensions of racialized fear: Such fear is rendered possible only by the social establishment of *discursive* frames which racialize perceptions of danger as associated with other human beings and, specifically, with crime.[8] (Such frames form historically specific conditions of possibility for the very perception of humans in terms of racial categories, in the first place.) Emotion – whether referred to as such or as affect or feeling –

---

upon by inchoate feelings that are not fully contained by those discourses' own terms of intelligibility" (see main text below). The idea that discourses enable and constrain what can be *felt*, as I have previously formulated it, is adapted from Michel Pêcheux's notion of "*discursive formation*" as being that which "determines '*what can and should be said* [...]'" (Pêcheux 1982, 111, emphases in the original; citing Haroche/Henry/Pêcheux 1971, 102). Foucault similarly (and, likewise, in rather structuralist coinage) characterizes the archive in terms of "the law of what can be said" at a given spatio-temporal conjuncture (1972, 129).

8   Hutta (2015, 300) states this point in similar terms. As the author remarks, "conceiving of viscerality as the generative site of affect per se and viewing semiotics as secondary mechanism of capture leads to reductive understandings of both body and language" (2015, 298). As I understand Hutta, such reductionism is characterized by a hierarchical opposition between affect (conceived of as primarily bodily) vs. semiotics or discourse, which the author critiques as much as I do here.

cannot, then, in any of its dimensions be disentangled from discourse when it comes to a subject whose very experience (including bodily experience) is constituted, as I maintain, by the terms provided by discursive frames or matrices of intelligibility. To the extent that this is disregarded, the discursive work that goes into the constitution of *anything* that can be felt or sensed by human subjects will be naturalized – and, thus, will be shielded from query and critical reflection. A *critical* theoretical account of affect/feeling/emotion must acknowledge its power-laden, and hence, its social character. It is in order to highlight the shared discursive dimension of emotion/affect/feeling, their entanglement with power relations, and the inseparability of the bodily aspects from the discursive aspects of this entanglement, that I use the terms 'emotion', 'feeling' and 'affect' interchangeably in this chapter; contrary to recent convention.[9] (I do so with reference exclusively to *human* subjects as discursively constituted beings.) Whether, despite these continuities, it makes sense to draw specific distinctions between the terms 'affect', 'feeling' and 'emotion' can certainly be debated, but is not the subject of this chapter.

The above in no way implies that what is felt can be *reduced* to the purely discursive. It is by recourse to a psychoanalytically inflected, poststructuralist notion of discourse as developed by Butler (amongst others) that we can safeguard a non-reductive account of the affective as exceeding the discursive, in the sense that it exceeds socially already-established matrices of intelligibility (see also Braunmühl 2012b). Due to the close association of affective life with power and its unequal social distribution, it makes much sense to posit – drawing on Butler's work – that the spectrum of discursive frames for emotional experience which is available at a given time and place is circumscribed by what may be termed its *constitutive outside*. As I have explained previously:

"The term, 'constitutive outside' refers to the fact that any discursive positivity that provides a matrix of intelligibility bases itself in a

---

9   See, e.g., Massumi (2002); Cromby and Willis (2016). Regarding Cromby's and Willis' article, see also note 5 to this chapter.

founding exclusion ('abjection') of what cannot be recognized or avowed as intelligible within the terms of that matrix (Butler 2003, 131; 1993, 3, 8, 22). This deconstructive re-signification of 'the unconscious' allows us to conceive of it (or of the psyche) as itself resulting from social/discursive processes, rather than as in any sense pre-discursive and an entity 'unto itself'" (Braunmühl 2012b, 224).[10]

I suggest that discursive scripts tend, on the one hand, to establish the possibility of feeling in particular ways at a given historical time and place – especially in ways that would stabilize hegemonic order, which tend to be biased in favor of legitimizing the social dominance of certain groups. On the other hand, such scripts tend to *abject* other ways of feeling as illegitimate, queer, or plainly inconceivable – particularly feelings which might threaten the persistence of hegemonic order. While, on this account, it is not possible to have feelings that are entirely unrelated to the spectrum of discourses operative at a given time and place, we can conceive of a transitional 'field' *between* what can be fully discursively articulated in a given social context and what can only barely be hinted at, yet which may make itself felt, for instance, in the form of symptoms in the psychoanalytic sense, or in an insistent sense of something missing in one's life, even if it seems barely to be specifiable what this might be. It seems to me that Butler has gestured at such an emergent, transitional 'domain' between what can clearly be stated and what it is impossible to say, when writing of a "critical perspective [...] that operates at the limit of the intelligible" (Butler 2004b, 107) as well as (with reference to subjects figured as only barely, if at all legible in terms of the binaries of gendered discourse) of "hybrid regions of [social, C.B.] legitimacy and illegitimacy that have no clear names, and where nomination itself falls into a crisis" (2004b, 108). From such "sites of uncertain ontology", according to Butler, there "[emerges] a questionably audible claim [...]: the claim

---

10   I here elucidate the notion of a constitutive outside as used by Butler. This notion is not exclusive to Butlerian theorizing, however, but has been used more widely within poststructuralist theory.

of the not-yet-subject and the nearly recognizable" (2004b, 108). In line with these allusions to what I understand as the notion of a 'realm' of discursive formation-in-the-making, we can thus posit that feelings may emerge *at the limits of discourse*, as associated with the abject and, ultimately, bordering on discourses' constitutive outside, their 'unconscious' – understood in the Butlerian, deconstructive-discursive terms referenced above. Emotions can then be conceived of as operating in significant part in terms of *unconscious* logics which – as with the notion of a constitutive outside, as deployed by Butler – are fully discursive in character, yet 'move' us in ways that may run up against, subvert, or even contribute to redirecting the logic of prevailing discourses, particularly with a view to the unegalitarian hegemonic norms entailed in these (Butler 1993; see Braunmühl 2012b for further detail).

This view assigns feelings an important role in struggles for political change. For, on the above account, it is partially at the limits of what is not (yet) fully speakable that affective life takes shape. This idea tallies with the notion that unegalitarian social arrangements – that is, being socially subordinated and considered a lesser form of human life than other such forms – occasion *emotional* costs (see above), from which a desire for change, and hence, resistance, may potentially emerge.

The Butlerian move of understanding discourses as being based in founding exclusions (which differ with each specific discursive formation [Butler 2003, 129–131]) offers the opportunity of theoretically tying 'discourse' and 'affect' into each other on the model of a chiasm – as an alternative to reducing either of these terms to the other or opposing them to one another dualistically. Thus, the above account entails that discourses not only offer frames for socially intelligible, legitimated feelings (promoting, eliciting, and positively shaping certain feelings over and against others by normative means) whilst abjecting (discouraging, stigmatizing or 'derealizing' [Butler 2004b, 27, 114, 217–218]) others. Rather, and in virtue of this notion, discourses can also themselves to a certain extent be given direction by feelings; in line with the Butlerian notion of abjection and the symptoms or resistances it potentially produces (Butler 1993). (I write "to a certain extent" because there can be no unmediated discursive 'equivalent' or 'expression' to affective experiences. Rather, the attempt to articulate any given experience involving feelings will in turn constitute the latter in terms of a given discursive frame, to the exclusion of other possible frames. I will return to this point further below.) That is to say, discourses shape and even render possible, in the first place, a certain, socially legitimated and fully articulable emotional repertoire (cf. Wetherell 2015, 147), but discourses must also be understood as themselves being potentially impinged upon by inchoate feelings that are not fully contained by those discourses' own terms of intelligibility – in line with the psychoanalytic resonance of the Butlerian notion of a discursive unconscious, understood as constitutive outside.

The chiastic model of the relationship between discourse and affect being developed here would not reduce affect to a conceptual addition to the notion of discursive practice, as proposed by Wetherell (2012; 2015). As indicated earlier, Wetherell's account of affective-discursive practice risks conceptually confining affect to a mere dimension of discourse. This is suggested by her move from the notion of discursive practice, proposed by her (with Jonathan Potter) in the 1990s (Wetherell/ Potter 1992), to the expanded but substantially unaltered notion of affective or affective-discursive practice (see esp. Wetherell 2012, 118–119; 2015, 152) – two terms she appears to use synonymously (2015, 152). 'Affective' here appears to figure as an add-on to the earlier concept, referring essentially to the *modality* in which discourses are practiced or performed. Wetherell writes (commenting upon William M. Reddy's [2001] concept of an 'emotive'):

> "I predict that *affective meaning-making* in most everyday domains might make, in fact, little distinction between 'emotives', and what we might call 'cognitives' and 'motives'. That is, speech acts formulating reasons and thoughts ('cognitives'), or action plans and goals ('motives'), will be as important as speech acts formulating emotions ('emotives'). *Affective-discursive action* is probably most frequently accomplished *seamlessly* through all three where it is more or less impossible to establish credible analytic distinctions between them.

[...] Just as affective neuroscience is *dismantling distinctions between affect and cognition*, those studying affective meaning-making *will perhaps need to do the same*" (Wetherell 2012, 73; emphasis added).

In Wetherell's account of affective-discursive practice, affect thus seems to be conceived of as an *accompaniment* to (or a property of) discursive practices, understood as contextually situated meaning-making (cf. Wetherell 2012, 76; 2015). There is no notion here of an affective life of discourses that would dynamize them, and give them direction, *as a function of their abjection of certain affects as unintelligible; as their 'unconscious'* (see esp. Wetherell 2012, Ch. 6).[11]

Due to the missing sense of dynamism in Wetherell's rendering of the relationship *between* discourse and feeling, her model of that relationship also would seem to be unable to account for change on a historical scale. For, her notion of 'affective-discursive practice' seems to be tailored primarily to the micro-level of social interaction, designating performances unfolding from moment to moment, i.e. in specific situations (see, e.g., Wetherell 2012, 72–74 and Ch. 4). By contrast, on the account I am offering here, the relationship between discourse and affect is conceived of in much more dynamic terms; in the sense that *each may act on the other*, and thus, in terms of a potential for *tension* between them: As suggested earlier, discourses may undergo historical transformation partially as a consequence of the insistence (in symptomatic or barely speakable form) of affects which the relevant discourses would nullify or fail to acknowledge – that is, ultimately, in virtue of the link I have postulated to pertain between *the emotional costs of social subordination or exclusion* to those negatively affected thereby, and

---

11   In her critical account of psychoanalysis, in which she rejects notions of what she calls "the dynamic unconscious" (2012, 123) as insufficiently social in conception, Wetherell very briefly mentions Butler's theoretical rendering of psychoanalysis, but fails either to endorse or to critique it (2012, 131). This is despite the fact that Wetherell's critique of psychoanalysis would barely seem to be applicable to Butler's *social-theoretical* reframing of the unconscious in terms of the concept of abjection (see main text above and below). Her remarks on Butler appear to be strangely unintegrated into her overall account.

a resulting *desire for (potentially political) change*. On this latter account, emotions abjected under a given hegemonic order – particularly as associated with social groups subordinated thereby – can contribute to the formation of new discourses. The theoretical bottom line here is straightforward: When discourse and affect are conceptualized as leaking into each other to the point of becoming indistinguishable, the possibility of dynamic tension *between* them becomes inconceivable.

Situating 'discourse' and 'feeling' in power relations: Towards 'double-edged thinking' (Butler)

I submit that to frame 'discourse' and 'feeling' as being chiastically related, as elucidated above, will in turn deepen our sense of 'discourse', providing us with a theoretically more grounded, politicized and more critical understanding of that term itself than what we have when we reduce discourse to verbal practices as they occur in specific situations, that is, to *what is empirically observable* (see, e.g., Wetherell 2012, 133–134, 75–76 and Ch. 3 more generally; see also Potter *et al.* 1990). To clarify what I find reductive about Wetherell's notion of a discursive practice – and insufficiently critical with a view to the saturation of both discourse and affect with power – I want to apply to this notion a critique that Butler has formulated with reference to an analogous notion of gender as performance, as reduced to activities observably performed:

> "It is not enough to say that gender is performed, or that the meaning of gender can be derived from its performance […]. Clearly there are workings of gender that do not 'show' in what is performed as gender, and to reduce the psychic workings of gender to the literal performance of gender would be a mistake. Psychoanalysis insists that the opacity of the unconscious sets limits to the exteriorization of the psyche. It also argues – rightly, I think – that what is exteriorized or performed can only be understood by reference to what is barred from performance, what cannot or will not be performed" (Butler 1997, 144–145).

As Butler goes on to argue, "certain forms of disavowal and repudiation come to organize the performance of gender" (1997, 145) – as in the collective melancholic repudiation of homosexual desire, which cannot be acknowledged and, hence, constitutes a lost possibility that is ungrievable as a matter of cultural proscription (Butler 1997, 145–148). As I understand it, the point made here by Butler incorporates an insight according to which power has positive, enabling *along with* negative sides to it, which must be considered together if we are to refrain from producing a foreshortened, one-sided notion of the term (see also Butler 1993, 8). A double-edged (Butler 2004b, 129) theoretical framing of 'power', in the sense just proposed, would do justice to the concept of biopower or biopolitics, as elaborated by Foucault (2004, Ch. 11) as well as Butler (2015a, Ch. 6): Either term in these writers' usage entails that the operation of power is bifurcated such that supporting, and protecting, the lives of some (e.g., 'straight' 'white' 'cis' people) is tied up with consigning others to physical or social death (e.g., queer People of Color). To think power as thus bifurcated entails the thesis that its negative operation for some subjects is constitutive of its 'positive' operation for others (Foucault 2004, Ch. 11; Butler 2015a).[12] As I read Butler, the significance of the notion of a constitutive outside, as she deploys it, is not limited to reconceptualizing the unconscious as discursive, as explained above. It is not limited to a psychoanalytic register. Rather, Butler uses this notion in a number of contexts, in such a way as to fruitfully articulate with each other *social* exclusion (groups of subjects consigned to social or literal death) and an analysis of the ways in which it plays out at a (collective) *psychic* level (see, e.g., 1993, 3, 8, 22; 2015a; see also Braunmühl 2012b).

When we think 'discourse' against the backdrop of such a double-edged conception of power (which is markedly critical in that it

---

12   Foucault's critique of the hegemonic construction of power as predominantly negative or oppressive led him to accentuate, for his part, power's productive or constitutive effects one-sidedly (see chapter 4 of this book). But the notion of biopower which he develops in *Society Must be Defended* (2004, Ch. 11) is more balanced.

highlights inequality) – that is, of power as both abjecting and constructive, and as simultaneously social and psychic in operation – then we will arrive at a richer, more complex understanding of the first term as well: If discourses are thought of as taking shape within the framework of generating their 'own' unconscious – a constitutive outside to the discourses in question – then they can be considered activities performed by subjects (as entailed in Wetherell's conception of discursive practice, with its focus on what subjects *accomplish* by way of "[a]ffective-discursive action" [e.g., Wetherell 2012, 73]) only *on the one hand. On the other hand*, subjects must then be thought of as *being* performed – constituted/abjected – by discourses at the same time (contra Wetherell 2012, Ch. 6). That is to say, from a double-edged notion of power, as such, we can move to an equally double-edged notion of *power as entailed in discursive practices*, according to which subjects both give shape to discourses and are shaped by them. This applies in the sense that what gets done when we engage discourses is far more than the effects we are aware of, let alone aim for (Butler 2004b, 173; cf. Braunmühl 2012b).[13]

Further, if we return, from here, to the relationship between discourse and affect, we can see how what, according to Butler, "is barred from performance, what cannot or will not be performed" (see above) in any given *discursive* practice is closely linked to the domain of *feelings* abjected by a given set of discursive scripts: It is *because* "what

---

13   Here I need to qualify my earlier account of the relationship between feelings and experience: I have previously written that emotions happen to us, 'doing' or even undoing us more than being done by us (Braunmühl 2012b). This was to produce as one-sided an account of the operation of emotions as Wetherell's account of affect as essentially an activity of subjects – only with a bias in the opposite direction. Today I would maintain that we need to hold on to both formulations at the same time. What is missing from the account I have given previously is the active, ethical dimension of subjects' relationship to emotions; the sense in which affective life is open to conscious influence, e.g., through the practices we engage in. To hold on to both of the above formulations at the same time would also be more consistent with the double-edged approach to theorizing the relationship between discourse and affect being proposed here.

is exteriorized or performed" (Butler, see above) *produces its 'discontents'* (Freud 1989) that the double-edged character of power, understood as biopower, entails that abjection as a process is affectively intensely charged. Indeed, *the discontents generated in virtue of the bifurcation of power is primarily affective in quality – rather than primarily cognitive.* On this view, power's negative side – its abjection of certain groups of subjects, in a simultaneously social and psychic sense – generates an affective charge that can account for the dynamic relationship I have posited to pertain between discourse and feeling: The emergence of new discourses becomes fully intelligible only when we understand the search for, or experimentation with, discursive alternatives (e.g., by social movements) to be motivated, first and foremost, *emotionally.* Such work at the boundaries of (already-constituted) discourse must be viewed as seeking to bring into the world, to establish as socially real and recognizable, what was previously derealized (Butler, 2004b, 27, 114, 217–218) or framed as unintelligible.

Ultimately, what I find missing from accounts of emotion, discourse and the relationship between the two which, like Wetherell's, reduce these both to an activity (2015) without considering the 'negative' implications of, or the shadows thrown by, what is 'positively' on display, is a sense of the affective costs of what discourses render as unintelligible and abject – of what they 'bar from performance' (Butler; see above). For the reasons detailed above, I find the Butlerian notion of discourses – namely, as steeped in abjection and, therefore, in melancholy or, put more generally, in an affective dynamic[14] – to be richer and deeper, as well as more politicized and critical, than the somewhat one-dimensional notions of discourse (including its affective

---

14   Butler in my view unnecessarily privileges melancholy and the associated subject of loss in theoretically framing the relationship between discourse and affect. While this is to take account of the biopolitical selectivity in terms of which hegemonic discourses frame only certain subjects' lives as grievable, while treating the lives of other subjects as ungrievable (Butler 2015a, 119), I believe that this forms only one of many different emotional repercussions potentially generated by discourses.

dimension) found in some cognitivist and praxeological accounts of emotion, such as Wetherell's or Eva Illouz's (2008), which may well be contained by a metaphysics of presence (Derrida 1976). These accounts lack a politicized sense of how *discourses* (organized as they are in terms of normative economies) *affect* subjects – in ways *both* enabling and disabling or destructive, that is, as potentially harmful at an affective level.

While I am arguing that feelings play a central role in struggles to form new discourses, the impact of feeling upon discourse can only ever be a mediated one, as alluded above: Any experience, however much it may be rendered as impossible or 'perverse' by extant discourses, can only be articulated by being framed in discursive terms. This process entails constituting such affective experience *in one way or another, to the exclusion of alternative* discursive possibilities and by reference to some form of *existing* discursive frame(s). It is in the course of 'citing' such frames that the latter are rearticulated and transformed over time: We can envisage *the manner in which* feelings can affect discursive, and thus political, change in terms of the Butlerian notion of "performativity as citationality" (Butler 1993, 12), as I have explained in more detail elsewhere (Braunmühl 2012b). Given that, as Butler argues with reference to the operation of norms, the law exists only in its citation (1993, 107–109), the citation of scripts for the socially situated (racialized, gendered, etc.) performance and experience of emotions is not necessarily a faithful, identical rendition of the normative prescriptions entailed in such scripts. On the contrary, 'outward' affective performance as much as the only *apparently* 'inward' attempt to 'feel the right way' can miss the mark, subverting and potentially even resignifying scripts for the performance of emotions, in sometimes unforeseeable ways.

Conclusions: From double-edged thinking to a practical politics of emotion

I submit that only if we conceive of discourses and emotions as potentially operating *in tension with each other*, as illustrated by the model of the chiasm, can we develop a theoretical account of their relationship which does not produce a hierarchy between the two, whether it be in the form of subordinating discourse to affect or the other way round. Once we consider both categories as implicating each other mutually, without either one being reducible to the other, we can envisage discourses as shaping emotions (without fully determining them), just as much as we can entertain the possibility of emotions affecting (without strictly determining) the form taken by specific discourses. That is, we can then conceive of the relationship between discourses and feelings in terms of *mutual* affectation – as contrasted with notions of a uni-directional influence that would seem to be hierarchizing at least implicitly.

What is more, we can then account, both for constellations of discourse and affect in which the two closely *cohere*, and for *dissonances* between them. This is so in virtue of the fact that, on the model introduced above, discourses shape affective life in terms of (implicit or explicit) normative distinctions between legitimate and illegitimate feelings, between emotions befitting or unbefitting a given category of subjects. Since those feelings which are socially legitimated and even promoted don't entirely exhaust the spectrum of what can be felt, however, there is scope *both* for feelings that cohere completely with already-available, fully articulated discourses, *and* for emotions that fail to do so in an absolute sense. It is politically important to provide for each of these possibilities at a conceptual level, as otherwise it would be difficult to account, on the one hand, for the formation of emotional and (eventually, in the best scenario) discursive as well as bodily *resistance* on the part of the socially subordinated and excluded and, on the other hand, for scenarios in which such resistance *fails* to form, due to an identification on the part of such subjects with the discursively prescribed, socially established emotional spectrum.

Theories of affect tend one-sidedly to highlight either the link between affect and subordination or between affect and resistance (see Bargetz 2015). Instead, both tendencies – the role of affect in cultivating compliance with relations of domination *and* its role in engendering resistance – should be thought of as always competing with each other, with either one outweighing the other at different times. Interpellation continues to be a useful notion when it comes to the evidence of widespread conformity, even submission, to hegemonic order (see, e.g., Braunmühl 2012a), including the feelings which the discourses associated with such order legitimize as compatible with it; as posing no threat. But what of those historical moments, and social tendencies, in which interpellation fails?

Arlie Russell Hochschild has made an apparently simple point which I find convincing as an explanation of the occurrence of resistance and movements for social change: She states (referencing Freud) that feelings entail a signal function to the self with a view to how a given state of affairs affects *me* (2003, 230–232; see also Hochschild 2003, 196–197). When she elaborates on the 'human' or 'psychological' *costs* of flight attendants' emotional labor (see note 2 to this chapter), her account harks back to the notion of such a signal function: It is because (contrary to some accounts) affects aren't free-floating entities unto themselves, but entail judgments as to the positioning of a socially situated *self* in relation to the rest of the world, that social subordination or exclusion generates suffering – at least as a tendency which, depending on how pronounced it is in a given context, potentially works against the force of interpellation. I find it utterly implausible to assume that resistance occurs primarily as a matter of *cognitive insight* into one's interests or into the injustice of the social order: If struggles for political and social change for the better (e.g., for equality) were not connected to the expectation that achieving such change would reduce suffering – the prospect of an "unbearable life or, indeed, social or literal death" (Butler 2004b, 8) – and would, by the same token, enhance the possibility of a livable life for all, then such struggles would be pointless.[15] The costs of subordination – aside from its material costs to those concerned, which are at least as significant for the formation of resistance movements in my view – are first and foremost emotional in kind (and this includes the ways in which subjects relate *affectively* to their perceived material interests and predicament). It is for this reason that struggles for hegemony involve a perpetually unstable balance of forces (Gramsci 1971), not only with a view to the relationship *between* opposing forces, but also to the *constitution of* counter-hegemonic movement – as part of which tendencies towards (self-)subordination compete with tendencies towards the contrary.

This returns us to the point with which I began this chapter: To theorize discourse, if it is to be a politicized endeavor (concerned

---

15   To say this is to disagree with Ahmed's claim that to strive for happiness, or to assume that happiness is what is good (i.e., desirable), is to operate in the hegemonic logic which she refers to as the moral economy of happiness (2010, 62, *passim*). In my view, a striving for happiness is necessarily entailed in the desire or impulse to escape affective discomfort (i.e. what *affects* me negatively), strong degrees of which I refer to as 'suffering'. Without taking such an impulse as given, much in our discourses – including Ahmed's (2010) theoretical discourse – would become unintelligible. For instance, if there were no connection whatsoever between social subordination, emotional discomfort, and the desire to escape it – however mediated and, hence, historically and culturally specific in modality we may take this connection to be – then the phenomenon of resistance would be unintelligible. I am suggesting, then, that we are dealing here with a necessary presupposition which we cannot possibly forego, except by way of contradicting ourselves. Ahmed does contradict the principal thesis of her book *The Promise of Happiness*, as paraphrased above, repeatedly when, in the same book, she uses terms such as 'happiness' or 'joy' affirmatively (see, e.g., Ahmed 2010, 69, 103, 114, 198; see also Ahmed 2010, 120). Rejecting particular (e.g. hegemonic) modes of framing 'happiness' does not require one to reject happiness as such. A more coherent approach would be to posit that all subjects strive for *some version* of happiness or 'joy', of being affected positively, however they may be framing what this is or entails. This is the case even when such positive affects are being sought in the experience of pain, as in masochism. The argument condensed in this note forms the subject of chapter 5 of this book.

with questions of power and inequality; in solidarity with struggles for progressive social change), makes it necessary to theorize affect at the same time. I have argued that a feminist and intersectional, egalitarian politics should move beyond hierarchizing accounts of the relationship between the two – whether such accounts be dualistic in the classical sense or identitarian. As a step in this direction, and in order to render with more precision a non-hierarchizing account of the relationship between feeling and discourse, I have proposed a chiastic model of that relationship.

In closing, I want to suggest that conceiving of affect and discourse as being chiastically related also has potential for the formulation of a feminist, egalitarian *practical* politics of emotion. Much like feminist *theory* (see, e.g., Ahmed 2010; Hemmings 2005; Bargetz 2015), such a politics would attend to the thrust, and the effects, of feelings (no matter whether these be categorized as such, as 'affects', or as 'emotions' by recent convention) with a view to their role in stabilizing unegalitarian social orders or in aligning with specifically progressive moves towards change. What is relevant about feelings from the point of view of a practical politics committed to social equality is to strive to *change ways of feeling that stabilize social hierarchy and exclusion*. This could include orienting to an ethos of non-identitarian integration (Braunmühl 2012b), which acknowledges the impossibility of governing or policing emotions exhaustively, whilst at the same time striving *mutually to approximate* our affective life and the discourses, as well as the norms, to which we orient (whether avowedly or merely implicitly [see Barnett 2008]) in struggling for political change.[16]

According to the line of theorizing developed above, this might entail orienting to feelings, and allowing ourselves to be guided by them, in our theorizing (that is, in re-fashioning discourses) – in much the way 'consciousness raising' has been conceived of, namely, as a collective labor of transgressing, and transforming,

---

16   The above is a modified version of the account of non-identitarian integration I have given previously. See notes 7 and 13 to this chapter for a fuller account of the change my thinking has undergone in this respect.

patriarchal discourse by attending to feminists' experiences (cf. Mardorossian 2002, 764–765, 769–771), including, presumably, their emotional experiences – while *at the same time* subjecting (our) affects to theoretico-political scrutiny and critique, thus seeking to re-orient them in light of the political norms we embrace. (For instance, as a way of allowing ourselves to be decentered as subjects positioned hegemonically in some respects in the face of political critique, when narcissism might instead prevent us from responding to such critique with solidarity, disposing us to react defensively or with paralyzing guilt instead.) We do not need to pick and choose between these feminist modalities of practically relating – by way of mutually orienting – emotions and discourse to each other. Rather than rejecting either of these two possibilities as incompatible with the other one, we can embrace them as complementary, as mutual correctives – thus rendering productive the tension between them.

4 Normalization/Normativity
In Disagreement with Michel Foucault, or: Taking Account of the Constitutive Outside

Preface

As noted in the Introduction to this book, it is far less common in the Anglophone context than in Germany or Austria to use the terms *normalization* and *normativity*, or *normalizing* and *normative*, as an opposition – at least within queer theory. In fact, it is more common in English-language queer theory to construe these terms as closely connected; often, with reference to Foucault's analyses of disciplinary power. Nonetheless, the critique developed in this chapter of the opposition found in publications in German between 'normativity' and 'normalization' has some pertinence for Anglophone queer theory, too. For, what is shared across these contexts is a distinctively dualistic pattern in dealing with what, in Foucault's own usage, was in fact a *three*fold distinction: In his lecture series at the Collège de France during the years 1977 to 1978, entitled *Security, Territory, Population* (Foucault 2007, 4), he differentiated the terms *normativity, normation* and *normalization* from one another where previously (e.g. in *Discipline and Punish* [Foucault 1991]) he had himself used only two of these terms, and had treated them largely interchangeably.

The dualistic pattern which I identify in the reception of Foucault – with a focus primarily on his queer-theoretical reception, which I consider politically more radical than, for instance, the governmentality school [1, 2] – is nowhere more apparent than in the following phenomenon: In both German- and English-language research associated with queer theory, which engages with the few pages in *Security, Territory, Population* on which Foucault introduces the conceptual distinction in question (Foucault 2007, 56–63), most writers focus on – or even mention, in the first place – solely *two* of the three terms he defines here, while ignoring the third term, largely if not entirely. In the writings in German upon which I focus in the main part of this chapter – which was originally published in German and addressed to a German-language discursive context – the term 'normation' has been ignored for the most part, while 'normalization' (or, alternatively, 'normalism') has been construed as a novel technology of power in contrast with 'normativity'. By contrast, within the mere handful of English-language publications I have been able to identify which engage the same passage in *Security, Territory, Population* from a queer-theoretical angle (or which take up Foucault's term 'normation', newly introduced here), it is the term 'normativity' that has been omitted by the majority of writers, who have given consideration only to the terms 'normation' and 'normalization' instead (McWhorter 2012;

---

1   Jürgen Link's theory of *normalism* (1998; 2013) – which forms a post-Foucauldian diagnosis or analytics of the present – has been received very widely in Germany, not least in radical political theory as well as queer theory. This is why I include a critical discussion of Link's work in the main part of this chapter, even though it is not itself queer-theoretical.

2   Amongst the references to the passage in which Foucault differentiates normalization from normation and normativity which have been published in English – and more generally, amongst the English-language references to the terms 'normalization' or 'normalizing' – I have been able to identify queer-theoretical rather than more explicitly queer-feminist texts. In contrast, some of the texts from the German-language context which I address in the main part of this chapter are more clearly queer-feminist – as well as antiracist – in orientation. It is this intersectional orientation from which I consider myself to be writing as well. In the main part of this chapter, I therefore make reference to queer feminism rather than (only) to queer theory in formulating a critique of Foucault (2007; 2010), Ludwig (2016b) and Link (1998; 2013).

Sauer *et al.* 2017; Amir/Kotef 2018; see also Chambers 2017[3] and –
writing without reference to queer theory, but following the same
pattern – May/McWhorter 2015; Kelly 2019). Obviously, to consider only
two of the three terms Foucault distinguished from one another as a way
of defining them is at the very least to pave the way for treating those
terms in dualistic fashion – if this move is not actually motivated, in
the first place, from within a dualistic sensibility.

As a caricature of this pattern, Sauer *et al.* actually mischaracterize
the term 'normation' as denoting sovereign power (2017, 107) – with
which Foucault had instead associated 'normativity'; a term Sauer
et al., too, omit.[4] To support this mischaracterization, they do not
even cite the only passage from Foucault's oeuvre in which the term
'normation' actually appears (Foucault 2007, 56–57), at least to my
knowledge. Instead, the only work by Foucault which Sauer *et al.*
(2017) cite is *The History of Sexuality*, Volume 1 (Foucault 1990), to
which the authors wrongly attribute both the terms 'normation' and
'governmentality' (neither of which is ever mentioned there). Such
binarization and misattribution of the differences which Foucault
outlined between sovereign or juridical power, disciplinary power, and
governmentality – with which he associated the terms 'normativity',
'normation' and 'normalization' respectively – certainly indicates a

---

3   Samuel A. Chambers (2017) mentions the Foucauldian distinction between
     all three terms, but fails to specify how Foucault defined normativity in the
     relevant passage, and how Foucault set apart both senses of 'normalization'
     from this first term (see below). This enables Chambers to omit the fact that
     Foucault defined "normalization in the strict sense" (Foucault 2007, 63) as
     basically non-normative, as we shall see. Chambers' own definition of the terms
     'normativity' and 'normalization' contradicts Foucault's in this regard; a fact that
     does not come to light in Chambers' account.

4   Sauer *et al.* further associate *'normation'* with a (right-wing) use of *"normative*
     human rights language"* (2017, 114; emphasis added). Normativity as associated
     by Foucault with juridical power is thus conflated with normation, as associated
     by Foucault with disciplinary power – a move which enables Sauer *et al.* to
     establish the following binary opposition: "Thus, while governing through
     normation is based on sovereign power, governing through normalisation is
     grounded in statistics and mean value." (2017, 107)

dualistic theoretical imagination. It is due to the need to question such dualistic tendencies in any variant that I believe this chapter is of interest to Anglophone audiences as well. Furthermore, illuminating certain differences between German- and English-language receptions of Foucault within queer theory, along with what is shared across these contexts, can contribute to de-familiarizing – and thus to de-hegemonizing – Anglo-American versions of such theory (and of 'Foucault').

Whereas in publications in German, 'normalization' (or 'normalism') has been opposed in sometimes dualistic fashion to 'normativity', in English-language texts which treat the pertinent passage from *Security, Territory, Population*, 'normalization' has been used, in several instances, in a meaning contrary to the one which Foucault gave it here – namely, to signify a (disciplinary) *deployment of norms* (McWhorter 2012; Chambers 2017; Kelly 2019, 2). This occurs despite the fact that, as we shall see in more detail in the course of this chapter, Foucault in this very passage defined "normalization in the strict sense" (2007, 63) in contrast to the neologism "normation" as *non-disciplinary*, in that – unlike normation or what he also referred to as "*disciplinary normalization*" (2007, 56–57; emphasis added) – normalization proper operates essentially in a manner *other than through norms*. As read by Meraf Amir and Hagar Kotef,

> "Foucault distinguishes between two types of normal (even if this distinction shifts and blurs at times). The first is the normal as it appears *within disciplinary apparatuses* [emphasis added] (such as mental disability or gender non-conformity). This 'normal' functions *in relation to a model, a pre-given standard* [emphasis added] of propriety, health, mental stability, identity, efficiency or productivity to which one should conform: 'the normal being precisely that which can conform to this norm, and the abnormal that which is incapable of conforming to the norm'. (Foucault, 2007: 85). The processes of measuring against this module and adopting [sic] subjects to it he then calls *normation* [emphasis in the original]. The second type of normal is that of biopolitics, which is, as Elden (2007: 573) observes,

'the means by which the group of living beings understood as a population is measured in order to be governed'. *This second meaning is devoid of judgement* [emphasis added], and is extrapolated from the calculated measurement of particular characteristics: here 'normal' marks a certain frequency of a trait and its location on a Gaussian curve, presumably reflecting the natural order of things. Accordingly, 'it is calculation (*calcul*). . . which is the model for these rationalities'; (ibid) [sic] rationalities that, in turn, are *connected both to liberalism and to security* [emphasis added] (and indeed the two often merge in the 1977–1978 lectures). *Within this domain 'normal' is not defined by a pre-given social model – marking a 'good' or a 'should' to which one must conform* [emphasis added] – but is *extrapolated* [emphasis in the original] from natural processes; *it is derived from empirical reality rather than being imposed on it in order to shape it* [emphasis added]. This, in short, is *the normalizing technology of security* [emphasis added]: a calculation of the frequency of a given phenomenon, which is inferred from the natural flow of things and living beings, their patterns of movement and modes of action." (Amir/Kotef 2018, 246–247)

While Amir and Kotef, too, simply ignore the third term defined by Foucault when he introduced the term 'normation' in contradistinction to 'normalization', leaving the term 'normativity' entirely unmentioned, I fully agree with them when they emphasize that Foucault considered normalization proper – unlike disciplinary normation – to be *"devoid of judgement"* (emphasis added) and, as such, *"derived from empirical reality rather than being imposed on it in order to shape it"* (emphasis added) (see quotation above). As my close reading of Foucault in the main part of this chapter will demonstrate in detail, this means that he considered normalization (as against normation) to operate in an essentially non- or post-normative manner – in accordance with neoliberalism which, as we shall see, he understood as essentially post-normative. It is this view of neoliberalism which I wish to problematize about Foucault, contrary to a widespread tendency to idealize his work as maximally critical.

While Amir and Kotef go some way towards deconstructing the opposition set up by Foucault between normalization as an essentially *descriptive* (statistics-based) mechanism of security, on the one hand, and normation as a properly normative, i.e. *prescriptive* disciplinary technology, they arguably do so in an ambiguous fashion that partially questions and partially affirms the above opposition. Certainly they do not critique Foucault for himself maintaining this opposition – a step I consider necessary as a way of specifying what, in Foucault's later studies of governmentality and neoliberalism, rather than in his earlier work on disciplinary power, is insufficiently critical when it comes to social exclusions that are based on what I hold is indeed *normative* about neoliberalism. My critique of Foucault is that his framing of neoliberal governmentality as essentially non-normative obscures its constitutive outsides – social exclusions which indeed continue to be based on pathologizing norms that abject some of us as 'abnormal'.

It is with a view to this necessary critique that the omission of the term 'normativity' from some of the few English-language texts in queer theory which attend to Foucault's distinction between 'normalization' and 'normation' (see above) assumes significance. As the third component of Foucault's threefold terminological distinction, the term 'normativity' was defined by him in terms of juridical power, understood as operating in negative terms of *pro*scription, and in binary fashion (Foucault 2007, 56, 46, 5). In this chapter, I argue that Foucault's juxtaposition of normalization (in the narrow sense associated with apparatuses of security and governmentality) against both disciplinary normation (defined by him in terms of *pre*scription, and hence, as involving norms [2007, 63, 57, 46–47]) and juridical normativity (2007, 56, 46–47, 4–6) chimes with his characterization of neoliberalism as devoid of pathologizing norms, as de-subjectifying, and as non-exclusionary. (This characterization occurs in the lecture series published under the title *The Birth of Biopolitics* [Foucault 2010], which he conducted between 1978 and 1979, immediately following his lecture series *Security, Territory, Population*.) It is via his *threefold* terminological distinction that Foucault marks out normalization as operating in an *essentially non-normative* manner, as we shall see –

contrary to his earlier understanding of normalization as *essentially disciplinary and, hence, as normative* (e.g. in *Discipline and Punish* [Foucault 1991]). This fact – this new, problematic development in Foucault's work – seems to have been ignored *throughout the queer-theoretical reception of Foucault within the Anglophone regions.* Amir's and Kotef's (2018) contribution here is singular and highly commendable in that it goes some way towards deconstructing the uncritical – indeed, the quasi-positivist – opposition between prescriptive normation and supposedly purely descriptive statistical techniques as associated with governmentality. However, as mentioned, Amir and Kotef do not critique Foucault himself for maintaining such an opposition, even though he clearly did, as my close reading of his lectures will demonstrate (see also the Postscript to this chapter).

Other writers on the subject either uncritically adopt Foucault's opposition between technologies of power presupposing norms vs. technologies of power supposedly devoid of any such presupposition, without problematizing its quasi-positivism, *or they do not take to heart Foucault's redefinition of normalization as non-disciplinary.* Thus, much like Gundula Ludwig (2016b), whose update on Foucault's diagnosis of the present will be in focus in my subsequent discussion of the reception of Foucault in the German-language context, so Shannon Winnubst (2012) constructs neoliberalism as having superseded a normative, juridical, identitarian rationality as previously analyzed by Foucault. (Winnubst does not actually cite *Security, Territory, Population,* but her reading of Foucault's subsequent lecture series *The Birth of Biopolitics* is clearly informed by the Foucauldian opposition between normativity vs. a neoliberalism which, like Foucault, Winnubst reads as "non-normative" [Winnubst 2012, 87]. This is why I include her text on Foucault, neoliberalism, and queer theory in this discussion.) In contrast, Ladelle McWhorter (2012, 72) has insisted (much as I do) that neoliberalism is indeed *normative*, but has ignored the fact that this claim cannot by any means be reconciled with Foucault's own words on the subject in the very passage at issue here, with which she does engage (McWhorter 2012, 66). Thus, she too fails to consider Foucault's very own definition of the term 'normativity' in contradistinction to 'normalization' and 'normation'. Surely this omission appears to be somewhat motivated, in that the contradiction between Foucault's words on neoliberal governmentality and McWhorter's own reading of neoliberalism as normative would require her to critique Foucault's analysis of neoliberalism along the very lines which I pursue in the pages that follow.

Whether one takes on board the uncritical aspects of Foucault's work on neoliberalism, governmentality and apparatuses of security (as distinct from disciplinary as well as juridical power), *or* whether one modifies its tenor in a more critical spirit while failing to note the discrepancy of one's own analysis from Foucault's: Either move adds up to an unnecessary idealization of his later work, which shields it from problematization and, hence also, from being developed further. I argue in this chapter that such problematization and further development is indeed necessary from an intersectional perspective, lest we take over from Foucault a euphemistic view of neoliberalism which obscures its constitutive exclusions. (As is hopefully clear by now, it is this risk that is at stake in Foucault's redefinition of normalization in contrast with normativity as well as normation, i.e. as essentially non-normative.) My own specific proposal for how to do so draws upon Foucault's own terminology (as well as on Ludwig's [2016b]), reframing it. There is no question here, then, of falling into the opposite extreme to that of an idealization of Foucault's work; of 'bashing' it instead. That would be, obviously, to maintain a dualistic either/or-ism (see Introduction, note 1) in which Foucault's tremendous contribution to our understanding of the present can only either be rejected wholeheartedly or be accepted uncritically, freezing it in time. Either approach to Foucault would obviously be as uninteresting as it would be unproductive.

A more productive reception of Foucault must of necessity be tuned to historical developments that occurred after his death. (The exclusionary force of neoliberalism, and its continued intimacy with binary, pathologizing norms is certainly even more apparent by the 2020s than it was at the time of Foucault's pioneering turn to the subject.) This has been one of the points made by writers in the field of queer theory who have warned that the latter needs to move beyond an understanding of power, and of heteronormativity, purely in terms of discipline or a juridical, identitarian normativity (Winnubst 2012; McWhorter 2012). Parts of queer theory have indeed neglected Foucault's later work on governmentality and neoliberalism, preferring to engage primarily *The History of Sexuality*, Volume 1 (Foucault 1990; see, e.g., Jagose 2015; Wiegman/Wilson 2015). Yet there must be an alternative to either producing an *opposition* between neoliberalism and disciplinary regimes or juridical power (Winnubst 2012, esp. 90; McWhorter 2012; Ludwig 2016b) or ignoring any differences between them entirely (whether by simply ignoring Foucault's more recent work per se, or by ignoring any differences he outlined between these various technologies of power [e.g. Chambers 2017; Kelly 2019]) in what is ultimately an identitarian logic. As indicated in the Introduction to this book, these alternatives, taken together, constitute a meta-dualism akin to the one identified by Lena Gunnarsson (2017) to pertain in debates on intersectionality: one in which either identity, affinity or continuity is given precedence over difference, or the other way round. Ultimately, a reception of Foucault's work which, in seeking to understand the present and its most recent history, privileges *either* 'discipline' *or* 'governmentality' at the expense of the other one of these *dispositifs* risks splitting apart power's productive dimensions from its more negative, coercive operations. (Much as occurs in Foucault's implicit construction of 'normalization', as associated with governmentality and apparatuses of security, in contrast to a 'normativity' which he defined as a modality of power operating *negatively* [2007, 46–49, 55–63]. As we shall see below, Foucault at the same time tended to identify the present predominantly with the first modality of power [2007, 8–11, 106–110].) This is reductive and politically problematic, as argued in the Introduction and, in more detail, in the course of this chapter. Rather than reinscribe any tendencies on Foucault's part to engage in dualistic splitting in this regard, doing justice to his genealogical approach with its emphasis on historical discontinuities *as much as* to the intersectional imperative to refuse to obscure the persistence of inequality, social exclusion, and other destructive operations of power – as Foucault unfortunately has tended to do in his work on neoliberalism

– requires us to read power's negativities and its productive effects *together*, as mutually *related*, yet irreducible to one another. (In a manner analogous to my proposal, in the preceding chapter, for conceiving of the relationship between discourse and affect, namely, in terms of the figure of the chiasm.) It is as a contribution to this project that the present chapter is intended. As such, it seeks to add to the rare instance of a 'queer' reception of Foucault's distinction between normalization, normation and normativity in which neoliberal and disciplinary power are read in terms of a *contemporaneous constellation* (Amir/Kotef 2018; see also May/McWhorter 2015; McWhorter 2017) rather than either as mutually exclusive (qua matter of historical succession) or as devoid of relevant differences.[5]

Introduction

Michel Foucault's distinction between normativity and normalization, understood as different technologies of power, has been incorporated into recent diagnoses of the present. In this chapter I aim to demonstrate that this distinction is deeply problematic from an intersectional perspective. For, this distinction incorrectly implies that normalization is post-normative. This serves to render invisible the social exclusions constitutive of neoliberal governmentality – which Foucault did indeed elide in his lectures on governmentality, in the course of which he introduced the said distinction (Foucault 2007, 56–63).

In order to substantiate this thesis, I will engage – on the one hand – with Foucault's distinction between normativity, normation

---

5   McWhorter's position in this regard has changed across successive publications. Whereas at an earlier point she asserted that disciplinary regimes and "networks for disciplinary normalization" are decreasing in significance (2012, 69), more recently she has analyzed neoliberalism and 'disciplinary normalization' – i.e. what Foucault referred to as 'normation' – in terms of a (changing) interplay (McWhorter 2017; see also May/McWhorter 2015, 254–255).

and normalization in a close reading. I will show that, with this distinction, he abandoned his earlier characterization of normalization as *fundamentally shaped by norms*, which in my view had been much more productive. On the other hand, I will demonstrate – by reference to Jürgen Link's work (1998; 2013) and, in some more detail, to the example of Gundula Ludwig (2016b) – that diagnoses of the present which take on board Foucault's later distinction between normativity and normalization thereby take on board as well the implication which I critique here: that normalization is non-normative (in the sense that it is free of evaluative norms). Finally, I argue that normalization is *constitutively normative*, pointing to Judith Butler's understanding of normativity in support of this argument. I propose to correct Ludwig's queer-theoretical diagnosis of the present through the thesis that, in neoliberalism, (hetero-)normalization and (hetero-)*normation* go hand in hand, operating *in normative fashion jointly, qua biopolitical tandem.* Throughout, I am concerned with a conceptual analysis of the relationship between normalization (or 'normalism' in Link's terms) and normativity, and with asking to what extent the (post-)Foucauldian terminology is adequate to a diagnosis of the present.

Diagnosing the present, with Foucault: normalization *versus* normativity?

Diagnoses of the present which draw upon Foucault's work at times oppose the terms 'normalization' and 'normativity' to one another whilst framing these terms as mutually potentially independent technologies of power (Ludwig 2016b; Engel 2002; see also Link 2013; Lorey 2011) – that is, as mutually independent at a conceptual level. In some cases this opposition operates as a dichotomy, whereby the third term which Foucault distinguished both from 'normalization' and from 'normativity' – the term 'normation' – is neglected (Ludwig 2016b; Bargetz/Ludwig 2015; Engel 2002). Some writers identify the present primarily with normalization (Ludwig 2016b) or, in the case of Link (2013), with what he terms 'flexible normalism' in contradistinction to a more rigid 'protonormalism'. (The latter term largely corresponds to the Foucauldian term 'normation' insofar as both of these terms are tailored to correspond closely to Foucault's analyses of disciplinary regimes [Link 1998, 266; Foucault 2007, 56–57].) All of the above needs to be questioned. In connection with doing so, I wish to take up the largely-ignored term *'normation'*.

I address Link's work here due to the widespread reception of his theory of normalism, which builds upon Foucault's oeuvre. I address Ludwig's text (2016b), and do so in somewhat greater detail, because Ludwig presents a relatively recent diagnosis of the present which in my view is especially apt – it is simultaneously queer-theoretical and antiracist – yet whose intersectional perspective is obstructed by the Foucauldian terminology which she uses, as I hope to show. My proposal for how to remove this conceptual obstruction – by reframing Foucault's tripartite distinction *normativity, normation* and *normalization* – can therefore fruitfully start out from Ludwig's contribution, building upon the terminology developed by her.[6]

---

6   In this chapter I refer to publications in German by Ludwig (2016b) as well as Link (1998; 2013), upon which the original, German version of my own text is based. Link (1998) is also available in an English translation (Link 2004) – unlike Link (2013). Ludwig's theoretical account (2016b) has been published in English in a somewhat similar version (Ludwig 2016a), yet which differs substantively in some details from her account in German, to which my critique in the main text relates. Accordingly, my critique of her account would be substantially similar if spelled out with respect to her article in English, yet would likewise differ in some details. Suffice it to indicate that I consider her article in English to be even more problematic than her article in German, in that it entails a fundamental self-contradiction. The article published in English concludes on the following note:
"As long as queer struggles fail to address sexualized, racialized, capitalist, neo-colonial biopolitics on a larger scale, the dynamics that Foucault has described as crucial for modern Western biopolitics in a capitalist society cannot be overcome: a dynamics that not only *divides humans into a group that is seen as worth of protection and a group that is framed as 'disposable'* but also a dynamic where the 'good life' of the former requires the (social) death of the latter." (Ludwig 2016a, 426; emphasis added).

As I point out in the main text, this intersectional perspective – which draws upon Foucault's *earlier* notions of biopolitics and of normalization – contradicts his *later* insistence that, unlike normativity as well as normation, normalization is non-binary. I suggest that these two (earlier vs. later) Foucauldian modes of analysis simply cannot be squared with each other since this would amount to claiming both that p and that non-p (see also note 12 to this chapter). Ludwig's attempt to combine them in her diagnosis of the present results in a self-contradiction in that, contrary to how her sentence, quoted above in this note, is framed – but in line with Foucault's subsequent redefinition of normalization – she claims that: "Heteronormalization is not built upon a binary of given norms and deviances, but instead it produces normality by integrating (some of) its deviances." (Ludwig 2016a, 423). As I argue in this chapter, (hetero-)normalization is indeed framed by a binary (i.e. bifurcating) dividing practice *in that* it operates in terms of a racializing biopolitics. Foucault's later notion of normalization as non-binary and post-normative (see main text) obscures this fact. In taking this notion on board as the basis for her own term, "heteronormalization", which she proposes to conceive of "as [n]eoliberal [t]echnology of [p]ower" (2016a, 422), Ludwig undercuts the intersectional perspective which she otherwise seeks to formulate – especially when, in addition, she identifies "flexible heteronormalization" as *the one*, prototypical technology of power in neoliberalism to the exclusion of a more "rigid", supposedly outdated, "heteronormativity" (2016a, 425). (Hetero-)Normalization can be framed as "flexible", not "rigid" only if it is inscribed as applying to 'whites' only. Indeed, it seems that gays and lesbians are inscribed as 'white' by Ludwig while racialized 'Others' are imagined as 'heterosexual' – in fact, it seems that she imagines the government of sexuality per se as a government of 'whites' – when she formulates as follows:
"The flexibilization of the apparatus of sexuality means that lesbians and gays as '"ordinary", "normal" citizens' (Richardson 2005, 519) have become part of the population whose lives should be optimized and proliferated whereas at the same time certain groups of people are rendered as 'disposable' – especially illegalized migrants" (Ludwig 2016a, 425).
This sentence comes close to emulating the hegemonic notion that "All the Women are White, All the Blacks are Men" (Hull/Scott/Smith 2015) – erasing from view queers of color and lesbian/gay illegalized migrants. In order to formulate a more rigorously and coherently intersectional perspective – which, likewise, draws upon Foucault, yet reframes his analytics of neoliberalism in line with queer-feminist and simultaneously antiracist concerns – I propose in this chapter that (hetero-)normalization must be analyzed as

I will now briefly introduce the terminologies used by Ludwig (2016b) and Link (1998; 2013), respectively, as related to the Foucauldian keyword 'normalization'. In opposing the terms 'normativity' and 'normalization' to one another in a Foucauldian sense, normativity is described as operating in a binary or dichotomous fashion (Link 2013, 33; Ludwig 2016b, 34); in contrast, normalization is said to operate on a "continuum of normality" ("Normalitätskontinuum") (Ludwig 2016b, 28). Normativity is characterized as a technology of power that categorically prohibits and sanctions (Link) or excludes (Ludwig) – with respect to sexuality, for instance, by way of categorically criminalizing and pathologizing homosexual practices and modes of existence. In contrast, normalization is defined as regulating 'deviations' from the mean value through partial adjustment; based on including a part of the previously stigmatized. Thus, Ludwig (2016b), starting out from Foucault's conceptual tripartition which juxtaposes normativity, normation and normalization, develops a distinction between 'heteronormativity' and 'heteronormalization'. In contrast to the first term, the second one denotes a flexibilization and "neoliberalization of the apparatus of sexuality" ("Neoliberalisierung des Sexualitätsdispositivs") (2016b, 43). Based on the example of the *Lebenspartnerschaft* (same-sex-partnership law) introduced in Germany in 2001, Ludwig characterizes heteronormalization as assimilating a proportion of the sexually 'deviant' to standards defined by a neoliberal majority society – for instance, concerning "the ideals of privatized relations of care inherent in heterosexual marriage" (Ludwig 2016b, 32; transl. C.B.). Her text is ambiguous with a view to whether the social operation of heteronormativity has been replaced

---

operating in conjunction with disciplinary (hetero-)*normation*, understood as an intersectional tandem of technologies of power which – contrary to Foucault's and Ludwig's claim that "normalization does not operate based on an a priori given binary norm" (Ludwig 2016a, 423) – *does* bifurcate the 'population' in binary, hierarchizing terms, and as such is constitutively normative in a sense which is indeed "a priori given", i.e. operative in advance of any statistical analysis. The above claim is deeply euphemizing and depoliticizing, as will become apparent in the course of the present chapter.

by heteronormalization entirely or only in part (Ludwig 2016b, 34–35, 39–41).

Largely in analogy with the term 'normalization', Link's term 'flexible normalism' describes 'normality' as a social frame of reference which, as Link avows, remains indebted – like the more rigid alternative, named 'protonormalism' by him – to normality's conceptual counterpart, 'the abnormal'. But, according to Link, the boundaries between 'normal' and 'abnormal' in the case of flexible normalism are fluid rather than fixed and impermeable, as they are in protonormalism: abnormality in flexible normalism is constructed as alterable and, therefore, as highly amenable to normalization (Link 2013, 207–208). Link considers flexible normalism within the global North since World War II to be culturally dominant (Link 2013, 108), but protonormalism in his view has not been fully displaced. He rather postulates a dynamic interaction between the two types of normalism which, in the future, might result in a shift from flexible normalism to a renewed dominance of protonormalism. Both variants of normalism are based upon statistical data processing and, as such, are specifically modern phenomena. *Normality*, Link maintains, accordingly is a question of descriptively specifiable degrees (as in a normal distribution curve) and, as such, differs essentially from the *normative* binary opposition between 'permitted' and 'prohibited'. The latter is found, according to Link, transhistorically in all societies and, thus, in modernity as well (Link 1998). However, he insists upon conceptually situating normality as well as normalism outside normativity – i.e. outside of norms (Link 1998, 2013, 32–34).

In my view it is misleading to oppose normalization (or normalism) to normativity – much as Foucault did so himself at one specific point (2007, 56–63). It is misleading insofar as that opposition suggests (in a manner which is itself remarkably dichotomizing) that *normalization is devoid of normativity at least potentially*. Contrary to this suggestion, I will argue that normalization *is constitutively normative* – a recent historical variant of normativity. This fact makes itself felt particularly to those who are *not* earmarked for inclusion within the framework of normalization. Most of the theorists mentioned (Ludwig 2016b;

Bargetz/Ludwig 2015; Link 2013; see also Lorey 2015) assert, after all, that only *parts* of those who previously were categorically stigmatized as 'abnormal' are normalized today. Yet, what about everyone else? Is an integration into the hegemonic social order in the sense of 'normalization' really available, for instance, to trans persons of color, and to the same extent as it is to 'white' lesbian or gay cis persons? The term 'normalization' as defined by Foucault in his lectures on governmentality (2007) is incompatible with a negative answer to this question, as I will demonstrate. The term 'normalization' is a misnomer, therefore, when it comes to technologies of power as they make themselves felt to those who are excluded from normalization partially or entirely. It particularly forestalls a thoroughly intersectional perspective.

"Who's Being Disciplined Now?"[7]

As Susanne Spindler (2006) argues in the context of racism, for minoritized subjects at the margin of the 'continuum of normality' – in the case of her analysis, these are imprisoned young migrants – other technologies of power take hold than they do for those who successfully distance themselves from such subjects (thereby successfully participating in normalization [see below]): For subjects in the first category, it is less a matter of the neoliberal mantra of responsible self-government and self-optimization than of overt repression, direct coercion and blatant subordination as well as exclusion (see also Tyler 2013; Haritaworn 2015). Spindler analyzes the racism to which these subjects are exposed such that they are excluded from neoliberal governmentality. With Foucault (2007), such technologies of power must be understood in terms of normation, as associated by him with discipline.[8] Similarly to Spindler, other writers

---

7   I here cite from the title of May/McWhorter (2015).

8   To this must be added technologies of power which Foucault might have classified as 'sovereign', even as they are not exclusively associated with state

have asked: "Who's Being Disciplined Now?" (May/McWhorter 2015). The various answers to this question add up to the view that discipline today applies (within the global North) to subjects of whom Foucault (1999; 2003) had already designated some as 'abnormals' in a critical spirit – such as psychiatrized and strongly handicapped persons (May/ McWhorter 2015) – as well as, framed in terms of class, to workers in the global South (May/McWhorter 2015) and the so-called 'dangerous classes' in the global North (Rehmann 2016; see also Hark 2000). Thus, Jan Rehmann writes:

> "[G]overnmentality studies overlook the fact that neoliberal class divides also translate into different strategies of subjection: on the one hand, 'positive' motivation, the social integration of different milieus, manifold offers on the therapy market; on the other hand, the build-up of a huge prison system, surveillance, and police control. The former is mainly directed toward the middle classes and some 'qualified' sections of the working class; the latter mainly toward the dangerous classes. According to Robert Castel [1991, 294, C.B.], today's power is defined by a management that carefully anticipates social splits and cleavages: 'The emerging tendency is to assign different social destinies to individuals in line with their varying capacity to live up to the requirements of competitiveness and profitability'" (Rehmann 2016, 152).[9]

---

actors (May/McWhorter 2015, 255–257). Todd May's and Ladelle McWhorter's designation of such technologies as 'premodern', and the fact that these writers partially locate the relevant practices outside neoliberalism, is problematic from a postcolonial perspective, however. We need to grasp the multiplicity of, and articulation amongst, technologies of power which operate in the neoliberal, global present in their contemporaneity; as (late) modern ones.

9   I cite from Rehmann's text (2016) with some hesitation since I find it rather polemical and even devaluing vis-à-vis some other writers. Nonetheless, I agree with Rehmann on those points concerning which I do cite him in this chapter.

'Normalization' in Foucault's analysis of disciplinary power

Framing technologies of power monolithically in terms of a single, dominant technology involves the risk that discrepancies in the social treatment of different categories of subjects, and between their respective social locations, will be obscured. From a queer-feminist and antiracist perspective it is essential, rather, to frame the social relationally, i.e. in terms of power *relations*, and thus, of differences. As Ann Laura Stoler (2015) and Megan Vaughan (1991, esp. 11) have made clear, Foucault gave little attention to systematic social distinctions amongst racialized and gendered groups of subjects (especially insofar as such distinctions are not confined to the framework of 'the nation', i.e. with a view to colonial relations of power). This applies all the more to the threefold distinction between normativity, normation and normalization which Foucault drew at one point in the course of his lecture series *Security, Territory, Population* (Foucault 2007, 56–63) (the first volume of his lectures on governmentality and neoliberalism). Therefore it is necessary to be especially cautious with a view to any attempt to characterize the present primarily in terms of normalization as a technology of power (see Ludwig 2016b, 41; Lorey 2011, 265–266) – something Foucault already did himself in connection with the said conceptual tripartition (see below).

Earlier on he had, however – more productively, in my view – analyzed disciplinary power as a form of power which operates via "techniques of socio-police division" (Foucault 1994, 75; transl. C.B.): "a permanent classification of the individuals, a hierarchization [...], the establishment of boundaries", where "the norm becomes the criterion for the division amongst individuals" (1994, 75; transl. C.B.), as Foucault had said as late as 1976. Even if he focused less on gendered and racialized norms than on norms related to illness/health, madness/sanity or criminality/conformity in analyzing disciplinary society, this analysis – conducted as it was in terms of "dividing practices" (Foucault 1982, 208) – did offer some purchase for reflecting upon the gendered and racialized dimensions of such practices as well: What I find decisive about Foucault's studies of disciplinary power is the relational emphasis of his focus upon the distinction 'normal/abnormal' (Foucault 2003). This emphasis makes it possible to attend to inequalities, hierarchizations and exclusions – in other words, to power *relations*. The relational emphasis of Foucault's analytics during this phase of his work was made possible by the fact that – unlike in his later lectures on governmentality (2007) – he did *not* set normalization, normation and normativity (understood in a wide sense of evaluation and directives for action) apart from each other. Instead, he emphasized precisely the value-laden character of normalization as a technology of power. Thus, in *Discipline and Punish* he asserted that what "*normalizes*" also "hierarchizes" and "excludes" (Foucault 1991, 183; emphasis in the original; see below for full quotation), and expressly related the term "normalization" – as well as the terms "[n]ormal" and "normality"– to the term "norm" (Foucault 1991, 184). Here he also spoke of "[n]ormalizing *judgement*" (Foucault 1991, 177; emphasis added), thereby emphasizing the evaluative character of normalization as he *then* conceived of it. And in 1976 he stated that: "We are becoming a society essentially articulated by the *norm*" (Foucault 1994, 75; transl. C.B.; emphasis added), specifying the meaning of a "society of normalization" (Foucault 1994, 76; transl. C.B.) *in this sense.*

Neoliberalism according to Foucault: post-normative and non-exclusionary

By contrast, Foucault in his lectures on governmentality develops a conceptual separation between normativity, normation and normalization qua different technologies of power which he represents as potentially mutually external (2007, 56–63). He thereby gives the term 'normalization' a new meaning which sets it apart from his earlier construction of this technology of power as fundamentally normative, i.e. value-laden and prescriptive. 'Normalization' is now redefined by Foucault as essentially value-free and non-prescriptive, as I will demonstrate in the next section. I offer the thesis that Foucault introduces this redefinition of the term 'normalization' on

account of the fact that he considers neoliberalism to have left behind
a normative, pathologizing division of individuals into 'normal(s)'
vs. 'abnormal(s)'.[10] In the present section, I will first demonstrate
this highly problematic transformation of Foucault's diagnosis of the
present.

This transformation is perhaps clearest in Foucault's remarks
concerning criminality (2010, 248–260). With a view to the genealogy
of neoliberalism he asserts in *The Birth of Biopolitics* (the second volume
of his lectures on governmentality and neoliberalism): *"Homo penalis,
the man who can legally be punished [...] is strictly speaking a
homo oeconomicus."* (Foucault 2010, 249; emphasis in the original).
Within a neoliberal grid of intelligibility, individuals qua potential
law-breakers are assumed to act rationally in line with a cost/benefit
analysis according to Foucault – an assumption which he takes to
be depathologizing. Thus he glosses the tenor of a 1975 text by Isaac
Ehrlich, whom Foucault refers to as one amongst a number of "neo-
liberals" (2010, 248):

> "In other words, *all the distinctions that have been made between* born
> criminals, occasional criminals, *the perverse and the not perverse,* and
> recidivists *are not important.* We must be prepared to accept that, in
> any case, however pathological the subject may be at a certain level
> and when seen from a certain angle, he is nevertheless 'responsive'
> to some extent to possible gains and losses, which means that penal
> action must act on the interplay of gains and losses, in other words, on
> the environment" (Foucault 2010, 259; emphasis added).

According to Foucault, taking the individual qua instrumentally rational
subject of an action as one's point of departure within a neoliberal grid
of intelligibility "does not involve throwing psychological knowledge

---

10   The original French title of Foucault's earlier lecture series "Abnormal" (Foucault
      2003) is in fact "Les Anormaux" (Foucault 1999) which, translated more strictly,
      would mean 'The Abnormals'. This 'substantivizing' French title drives home
      the essentializing disqualification of those labeled as 'abnormals', i.e. abnormal
      subjects, even more clearly than its English rendering as an adjective.

or an anthropological content into the analysis" (2010, 252). "This also means that in this perspective the criminal is not distinguished in any way by or interrogated on the basis of moral or anthropological traits. The criminal is nothing other than absolutely anyone whomsoever. *The criminal, any person, is treated only as anyone whomsoever* who invests in an action, expects a profit from it, and who accepts the risk of a loss. [...] *The penal system itself will not have to deal with criminals*, but with those people who produce that type of action" (Foucault 2010, 253; emphasis added) – meaning that, as Foucault concludes: "there is an anthropological erasure of the criminal." (Foucault 2010, 258)

These remarks by Foucault could lead one to conclude that, when it came to neoliberalism, he no longer deemed social exclusion, as associated with the stigmatizing pathologization of certain social groups, to be relevant. Is *discrimination* – for instance, based upon racism or heteronormativity – even thinkable when the neoliberal approach to crime is characterized along these lines? Doesn't this characterization obscure discrimination qua institutionalized practice that fundamentally shapes the criminal justice system (Braunmühl 2012a; Spindler 2006)? In my view, the latter is indeed the case: Social inequalities, which registered in Foucault's earlier analysis of disciplinary power in terms of an exclusionary division between 'normals' and 'abnormals' (Foucault 1999; 2003), are rendered systematically invisible by his account of neoliberal governmentality. This is due to its unitized, non-relational character, which fails to attend to differences between the hegemonic treatment of dominant vs. minoritized categories of subjects. The claim that, in a neoliberal perspective, "[t]he criminal is nothing other than absolutely anyone whomsoever" and "is treated only as anyone whomsoever" (see quotation above) is downright suggestive of an equal treatment of all, as if discrimination were unknown within neoliberalism. Accordingly, Foucault expressly states:

> "you can see that what appears on the horizon of this kind of [neoliberal, C.B.] analysis is not at all the ideal or project of an exhaustively disciplinary society in which the legal network hemming

in individuals is taken over and extended internally *by, let's say, normative mechanisms. Nor is it a society in which a mechanism of* general normalization and *the exclusion of those who cannot be normalized is needed.* On the horizon of this analysis we see instead the image, idea, or theme-program of a society in which there is an optimization of systems of difference, in which the field is left open to fluctuating processes, *in which minority individuals and practices are tolerated,* in which action is brought to bear on the rules of the game rather than on the players, and finally in which there is an environmental type of intervention *instead of the internal subjugation of individuals."* (Foucault 2010, 259–260; emphasis added)

This passage unmistakably clarifies that Foucault considers the neoliberal approach to crime as he characterizes it to be *non-normative* and even straightforwardly non-subjugating. *An exclusion of those who cannot be normalized is not needed,* as stated explicitly in the passage just quoted.

'Normalization' in *Security, Territory, Population*: post-normative

Judging from how Foucault constructs the term 'normalization' in *Security, Territory, Population* (2007) in distinction from 'normation' as well as 'normativity', he understands not solely neoliberalism, but also and especially 'normalization' as post-normative in a certain sense, and thus implicitly – in line with his remarks upon neoliberalism as considered above – as non-exclusionary; at least with a view to social exclusions that put to work hierarchizing and pathologizing norms. In my view, this fact renders the distinction between 'normalization', 'normation' and 'normativity' as drawn by Foucault unproductive and deeply problematic for the purposes of a queer-feminist, antiracist diagnosis of the present. For, ultimately, the said distinction results in a denial of pathologizing forms of social hierarchization and exclusion – in stark contrast to the elementary concerns of both antiracism and queer feminism. This happens by way of a unitizing analysis which suggests either that societies of the present are no longer organized in terms of social exclusions which operate on the basis of norms, or that such exclusions are no longer relevant to a diagnosis of the present.

This is exactly the theoretico-political thrust of the term 'normalization' as developed by Foucault in *Security, Territory, Population* in contradistinction both to 'normation', as associated by him with discipline, and to 'normativity' – the meaning of which term he confines to the operation of the law (2007, 56). This restriction unduly narrows the meaning of 'normativity' in a manner that is depoliticizing insofar as it fails to recognize as 'normative' forms of normative assessment – i.e., forms of assessment that involve norms – other than those associated with the law. The value-laden character of such non-legal forms of normativity is thereby rendered invisible. According to Foucault, normativity as associated with the law is a negative technology which operates in terms of a binary distinction between what is permitted and what is prohibited (Foucault 2007, 46, 5–6) – much as in Link's and Ludwig's accounts (see above). By contrast, discipline on Foucault's account operates via the norm in a prescriptive sense: while the law prohibits, discipline prescribes (2007, 47). Foucault coins the term '*normation*' for a modality of power that involves norms, which he had already analyzed in terms of disciplinary power in the past (2007, 56–57; see above). That is to say, he understands 'normation' as a relational and hierarchizing differentiation between 'normal' and 'abnormal' which is shaped by norms in the sense that it is value-laden and entails prescriptions for conduct (whether explicitly or implicitly). Put in Foucault's own words,

> "discipline fixes the processes of progressive training (*dressage*) and permanent control, and finally, on the basis of this, it establishes the division between those considered unsuitable or incapable and the others. That is to say, on this basis it divides the normal from the abnormal. Disciplinary normalization consists first of all in positing a model, an optimal model that is constructed in terms of a certain result, and the operation of disciplinary normalization consists in

trying to get people, movements, and actions to conform to this model, *the normal being precisely that which can conform to this norm, and the abnormal that which is incapable of conforming to the norm*. In other words, it is not the normal and the abnormal that is fundamental and primary in disciplinary normalization, it is the norm. That is, *there is an originally prescriptive character of the norm* and the determination and the identification of the normal and the abnormal becomes possible in relation to this posited norm. *Due to the primacy of the norm in relation to the normal*, to the fact that disciplinary normalization goes from the norm to the final division between the normal and the abnormal, I would rather say that what is involved in disciplinary techniques is a normation (*normation* [emphasis in the original]) *rather than normalization*. Forgive the barbaric word, *I use it to underline the primary and fundamental character of the norm*." (Foucault 2007, 57; emphasis added)

In other words, Foucault now understands the term 'normation' in the very way in which, in *Discipline and Punish*, he had used the term '*normalization*' in general (1991, 182–184). In his subsequent lecture series entitled *Security, Territory, Population*, by contrast, he draws a distinction between – on the one hand – 'normation', which he also refers to as "disciplinary normalization" (Foucault 2007, 56–57; see quotation above) and – on the other hand – "normalization in the strict sense" (Foucault 2007, 63), which he identifies with the apparatus of security (Foucault 2007, 57–63). It is this apparatus that he now wants to study (2007, 6). By the time of this lecture series, Foucault tends to assess *security* as the dominant technology of power in the present (2007, 8–11, 106–110); as the essential technical instrument of a governmentality in whose "era" we live according to him (2007, 108–109) – that is, in a "society controlled by apparatuses of security" (Foucault 2007, 110). (Whereas only two years earlier, he had diagnosed that: "We are becoming a society essentially articulated by the *norm*" [Foucault 1994, 75; transl. C.B.; emphasis added], as we saw above – i.e. in terms of what, by 1978, he would rename as 'normation' as opposed to 'normalization in the strict sense'.) Foucault determines apparatuses of security to be *non-prescriptive*:

> "In other words, the law prohibits and discipline prescribes, and the essential function of security, *without prohibiting or prescribing*, but possibly making use of some instruments of prescription and prohibition, is to respond to a reality in such a way that this response cancels out the reality to which it responds – nullifies it, or limits, checks, or regulates it. I think this regulation within the element of reality is fundamental in apparatuses of security." (Foucault 2007, 47; emphasis added)

Since Foucault describes the mechanism of security to which he assigns the notion of a 'normalization in the strict sense' as non-prescriptive (see also Foucault 2007, 45, 46), while simultaneously emphasizing that he chooses the term 'normation' due to the centrality of norms to this latter technology, from which he sets apart the technology of 'normalization in the strict sense' (Foucault 2007, 57; see above), this means that he considers 'normalization in the strict sense' to be tied to norms – understood as what is value-laden – less fundamentally than normation.[11] This is also confirmed directly by how Foucault defines 'normalization in the strict sense':

> "We have then a system that is, I believe, exactly the opposite of the one we have seen with the disciplines. *In the disciplines one started from a norm*, and it was in relation to the training carried out with reference to the norm that the normal could be distinguished from the abnormal. Here, instead, we have a plotting of the normal and the abnormal, *of different curves of normality*, and the operation of normalization consists in establishing an interplay between these different distributions of normality and [in, *translator's note*] acting to bring the most unfavorable in line with the more favorable. So we have here something that *starts from the normal* and makes use of certain

---

11   Isabell Lorey, too, reads Foucault in this way (2011, 280–281, 275, n. 136), as do
      Amir/Kotef (2018) (see Preface and Postscript to this chapter).

distributions considered to be, if you like, *more normal than the others,* or at any rate more favorable than the others. *These distributions will serve as the norm.* The norm is an interplay of differential normalities. *The normal comes first and the norm is deduced from it,* or the norm is fixed and plays its operational role *on the basis of this study of normalities.* So, I would say that what is involved here is no longer normation, but rather normalization in the strict sense." (Foucault 2007, 63; emphasis added)

According to this passage, Foucault does view "normalization in the strict sense" as involving a norm. But unlike in the case of normation, in normalization in the strict sense he views the norm as secondary vis-à-vis "a plotting of the normal and the abnormal" which he casts as *descriptive* rather than prescriptive – as Sushila Mesquita too observes (2012, 46; see also Amir/Kotef 2018). Foucault thereby sets apart a normality which purportedly is measurable in an initially merely descriptive sense from a normation which, by contrast, he considers to be constitutively determined by prescriptive, evaluative norms and assigns to disciplinary regimes (see above). In doing so, he naturalizes the intrinsically value-laden character of any possible distinction between 'normal' and 'abnormal'. He thus renounces his earlier, politicizing and – therefore – more productive conception of normalization as being fundamentally shaped by norms (and as normative *in this sense*). This makes it impossible to take account of the hierarchizing, exclusionary character of any possible notion of 'normality'. (Any possible notion of 'normality' is exclusionary in virtue of the constitutive relationship of this term to its stigmatizing, devaluing counterpart, the 'abnormal', as I will argue below.) This step, which Foucault undertakes in the first of his two consecutive lecture series on governmentality and neoliberalism (2007), corresponds to his negation of neoliberalism's exclusionary character, discussed above, in the second lecture series on these subjects (Foucault 2010): With his redefinition of the term 'normalization' in contrast to the terms 'normation' and 'normativity' he paves the way for his thesis, treated above, according to which the neoliberal project can do without pathologizing, exclusionary divisions of 'normal vs. abnormal' at least in the context of crime. I now want to address a second case in point on which I base my reading of Foucault along these lines, i.e. as denying the exclusionary parameters of neoliberalism: a significant change in his understanding of biopolitics, as articulated in the second of the said two lecture series – *The Birth of Biopolitics* (2010).

Biopolitics and neoliberalism: post-racist?

In his earlier lecture series *Abnormal*, Foucault (2003, 291–321) had related 'abnormality' to theories of heredity and had analyzed them as a form of racism. In his next lecture series, *Society Must Be Defended* (Foucault 2004, 239–264), he developed a notion of biopolitics or biopower according to which the protection and optimization of the lives of some is *based upon* the annihilation of others – whether literally or through indirect forms of murder. Foucault explicitly turns away from this notion of "biopolitics" (2004, 243), which was still shaped entirely by the idea that it is framed by practices that *divide* subjects (a "caesura" [2004, 255]) in accordance with the opposition 'normal vs. degenerate', in *The Birth of Biopolitics* (Foucault 2010, 227–229). Here he thus abandons his earlier – short-lived (cf. Stoler 2015, 333) – analysis of racism as constitutive of modern and contemporary societies (Foucault 2004, 254–263). In the context of his account of American neoliberalism and its reframing of *homo oeconomicus* as entrepreneur of himself, he maintains that, in the present, "the political problem of the use of genetics arises in terms of the [...] improvement of human capital" (Foucault 2010, 228) – for instance, in the context of genetic risk factors which might play a role in selecting a spouse or co-producer for reproductive purposes – *and not* as a question of racism (Foucault 2010, 227–229). In *The Birth of Biopolitics*, Foucault states:

> "What I mean is that if the problem of genetics currently provokes such anxiety, I do not think it is either useful or interesting to translate this anxiety into the traditional terms of racism. If we want to try to grasp the political pertinence of the present development of genetics,

we must do so by trying to grasp its implications at the level of actuality itself, with the real problems that it raises [sic]. As soon as a society poses itself the problem of improvement of its human capital in general, it is inevitable that the problem of the control, screening, and improvement of the human capital of individuals, as a function of [sexual/marital, C.B.] unions and consequent reproduction, will become actual, or at any rate, called for. So, the political problem of the use of genetics arises in terms of the formation, growth, accumulation, and improvement of human capital. What we might call the racist effects of genetics is certainly something to be feared, and they are far from being eradicated, but this does not seem to me to be the major political issue at the moment." (2010, 228–229)

Here Foucault clearly uncouples biopolitics (as it obviously plays into the subject of these remarks) from racism. These remarks demonstrate that, at the time of his lectures on governmentality and neoliberalism, Foucault no longer considered racism to be constitutive of biopolitics, at least not in the present. At the same time, the above quotation implies that Foucault dissociates *neoliberalism* from racism, for (American) neoliberalism and specifically the neoliberal theory of human capital form the immediate context of his just-cited remarks. I regard this as providing further evidence supporting my thesis that, on Foucault's conception of neoliberal governmentality, exclusion no longer plays a decisive or politically important role with respect to it. This corresponds exactly to the politico-theoretical thrust of his account of the neoliberal approach to crime, on the one hand, and his distinction between normativity, normation and normalization, on the other, as analyzed above. My conclusion from Foucault's remarks as examined above, then, is this: It is part of the very sense of his distinction between 'normativity', 'normation' and 'normalization' to construct the latter as post-normative and, in virtue of this, as no longer in need of mechanisms of excluding 'the abnormal'.

While it would unduly disambiguate Foucault's work to argue that he either exclusively legitimized or exclusively critiqued neoliberalism (Zamora/Behrent 2016; Lorey/Ludwig/Sonderegger 2016), I do find it necessary to assert that he smoothed out all tension between neoliberal rhetoric and the actual operation of neoliberalism (see note 13 to this chapter; see also Duggan 2004, 18; Rehmann 2016, 143–144, 148), and that he thereby exposed himself to the risk of taking on board neoliberalism's euphemizing construction of itself. This applies especially with a view to the question of whether neoliberalism or the apparatuses of security advance normative hierarchizations and social exclusion or not – as is evident from Foucault's words, as cited above. In denying this, his analysis of neoliberalism promotes the tendency of the latter to dissimulate its own violence (which, by contrast, is emphasized by Ludwig [2016b, 25–27]). In the next section, I want to demonstrate, based upon the example of Ludwig (2016b), that taking over Foucault's distinction between normalization and normativity for the purposes of a diagnosis of the present is to run the risk of reinscribing the euphemistic character of his notion of normalization as non-normative and devoid of norms in a prescriptive-evaluative sense.

'(Hetero-)Normalization' and intersectionality

Ludwig elucidates the concept of heteronormalization, starting out from the distinction made by the later Foucault between normalization, normation and normativity, as follows: According to her, a privileged part of the formerly categorically excluded sexual minorities today is offered social integration on neoliberal parameters, while groups racialized as 'Other' – whether sexually minoritized or not – continue to be socially excluded. The social integration of 'white' gays and lesbians – which other queer theorists have described in terms such as (for instance) *homonormativity* (Duggan 2004) or projective integration (*projektive Integration*) (Engel 2009) – takes place, then, at the expense of subjects excluded on the basis of racism; as a process of 'white' lesbians' and gays' refusal of solidarity. This analysis contradicts Foucault's account of neoliberalism and of the term 'normalization' as post-normative and non-exclusionary, as examined above with regard to his lectures on governmentality and neoliberalism (2007; 2010). It also ignores the crucial transformation which Foucault's notion of biopolitics undergoes within these lectures, in which he forsakes his earlier thesis that racism is constitutive of modern and contemporary societies (Foucault 2004, 243, 254–263), as we have seen.[12]

The effect, indicated above, of a dissimulation of neoliberalism's violence on Foucault's part – which corresponds conceptually to his definition of 'normalization' as non-normative – is in turn reinscribed by Ludwig in symptomatic fashion, even though I am certain that this is contrary to her intentions. Symptomatically for the euphemism entailed in Foucault's later usage of the term 'normalization' – namely, for the notion that normalization qua technology of power is non-normative – the structure of Ludwig's article (2016b) militates against a thoroughly intersectional perspective: Her analysis of the government of sexuality in terms of the concept of heteronormalization, modeled as it is on Foucault's terminology, in the (middle) part of her text within which this this concept is introduced and contextualized (Ludwig 2016b, 29–36) privileges the dimension of sexuality while largely ignoring racism. Arguably, this forms the condition of possibility for

---

12   Ludwig (2016b, 17–19, 41–43) refers to Foucault's earlier remarks on racism to support her reading of Foucault's term 'normalization' in line with her own antiracist theoretical framework. Years earlier, Foucault had analyzed racism as a constitutive moment of biopower; namely, in *The History of Sexuality*, Volume 1 (1990) and in his lecture series *Society Must Be Defended* (2004). However, as argued above, Foucault's own later remarks in his lectures on governmentality and neoliberalism are at odds with this critical notion of biopolitics. By this I mean not merely his remarks about neoliberalism, but also specifically about the term 'normalization' as well as about racism (see above). In my view, moreover, there is nothing to be found either in *Security, Territory, Population* or in *The Birth of Biopolitics* that would support a reading of Foucault according to which his earlier, critical, antiracist notion of biopolitics coheres with his later analysis of neoliberalism in general and normalization in particular. I see a radical discrepancy, therefore, between the latter analysis and the antiracist intention underpinning Ludwig's analysis of heteronormalization as a fundamentally racialized technology of power. As argued in the main text, her intention is partially thwarted by her use of the Foucauldian terminology as shaped by Foucault's views on neoliberalism. See also note 6 to this chapter.

Ludwig's rendering of heteronormalization in terms of a *flexibilization* of the apparatus of sexuality (see above). Only in a further part of her article does Ludwig (2016b, 39–43) assert that the neoliberal *inclusion* of lesbians and gays into the societal mainstream – i.e., heteronormalization – operates as an offer of integration to '*white*' (and, as would need to be added in my view, middle- and upper-class) gays and lesbians *and not* to racialized minorities. Considering this thesis, which in terms of the structure of Ludwig's article is added only belatedly to her account of the term '(hetero-)normalization', the latter term turns out to be a misnomer in that it is introduced as a *global* technology of power rather than a technology addressed selectively to relatively privileged queers; namely, to 'white' members of the middle and upper classes and – it must be added – even amongst these, possibly only to those who are neither inter nor trans nor (being) handicapped nor subjected to psychiatric 'treatments'. In other words, Ludwig describes the neoliberal government of sexuality *in general* by the term 'heteronormalization' – as if it could also be used to apply to the 'government' of those subjects of whom she writes herself that their social integration is not envisaged; on whose backs heteronormalization operates as an offer of integration specifically to 'white' gays and lesbians (2016b, 39–43). Yet how could this term possibly designate an *exclusion* of subjects when, to the contrary, it connotes an *assimilation* to the standards of majority society – a technology of making-normal, as Link puts it (2013, 10–11) – and when it is elaborated in just this way by Ludwig (following Foucault) (Ludwig 2016b, 29–36)? Especially given that Ludwig distinguishes heteronormalization on exactly this count from a hetero*normativity* which she defines as exclusionary, and of which she writes at one point that, in neoliberalism, it has been replaced by heteronormalization qua technology of power (Ludwig 2016b, 34–36, 41)? By definition, 'normalization' as a technology of power can apply only to those subjects who, hegemonically, are regarded as 'able to integrate' and 'optimizable'. *This is why a universalizing use of the term '(hetero-)normalization' in the sense of 'the' one or the main neoliberal technology of power covers over the disciplining of subjects who are not accorded such assessment. It contributes at the level* *of political theory to rendering the hegemonic treatment of such subjects and their social positionalities invisible, that is, subaltern.* I consider such use of the term '(hetero-)normalization' to entail violence, which is certainly unintended by Ludwig, yet which inheres in the term 'normalization' when it is used in such a way as to qualify it as 'the' (dominant) neoliberal technology of power, i.e. as applying 'across the board' – as conceived by Foucault. It should become clear that this term as he characterized it in connection with apparatuses of security, governmentality and neoliberalism is incompatible with an intersectional analysis of the government of sexuality which attends to racism and other axes of power from the very first, as soon as one asks: How are queers of color and other marginalized queers 'governed' – when it comes to sexuality and otherwise (see, e.g., Haritaworn 2015) (see also note 6 to this chapter)? This question in turn raises the question: With what further technologies of power is "heteronormalization" associated?

But even if one does not designate heteronormalization as the dominant or even the only technology of governing sexuality within neoliberalism (as Ludwig does at one point in her essay [2016b, 41]) but instead restricts oneself to advancing the thesis that heternormalization has joined heteronormativity as a further technology of power (see Ludwig 2016b, 34–35), even this would be politically problematic. For – contrary to how the latter thesis, as formulated by Ludwig, can be understood – both modes of government do not co-exist contingently by any means, as mutually independent technologies. Rather, according to the principle of intersectionality "(hetero-)normalization" and "(hetero-)normativity" as defined by Ludwig would need to be understood *relationally*, in the sense that they form systematically connected – more specifically: intertwined – discriminatory *dividing practices* (see above). Within their bifurcating framework, different categories of subjects are exposed to what tend to be diverging technologies of power: Whereas normalization targets primarily subjects who, from an intersectional perspective, tend to be positioned hegemonically, for other subjects, techniques associated with normation remain at least as virulent as the technology of normalization – insofar as subjects exposed to normation are addressed by normalizing interpellations *at all* at the same time.[13] (This is questionable, for instance, for the jailed young migrants whose exclusion from governmentality Spindler analyzes [2006].)

For this reason it would be more coherent to juxtapose heteronormalization to a further technology of power named hetero*normation*, whilst conceptualizing both technologies of power as *constitutively normative* (not least as hetero-normative), as detailed in the following section. To instead frame hetero*normativity* as one technology of power amongst others, such as heteronormalization – as Ludwig does – is to suggest incorrectly, if true to Foucault, that normalization is *not* normative.

No 'normality' without 'the abnormals'

As soon as one understands technologies of power relationally and intersectionally as plural as well as mutually constitutively intertwined – and for the purposes of a diagnosis of the present, as a biopolitical *tandem involving normalization for some and normation for others* – it becomes clear that *both* technologies of power are constitutively

---

13   Beside other technologies of power, most subjects in neoliberalism may be addressed as well by normalization *to a certain extent* (cf. Engel 2002, 78, 80). But I wish to emphasize that the extent to which subjects can find themselves '*intended*' by normalizing interpellations varies strongly by social location. With subjects who, from an intersectional perspective, tend to be socially subordinated more than superordinated, neoliberal technologies of power can register through a contradictory constellation of interpellations: The promise that one can be normalized, which may animate attempts to self-optimize, here coexists with messages according to which the subjects concerned are *inapt* in a biopolitical sense (Foucault 2004, 239–264) – *and, as such, unsuitable – for optimization*. There is thus a discrepancy between the rhetoric of equal opportunity and an experience of impermeable boundaries which remain shaped to a strong degree by axes of social inequality such as gender and racism. In asserting this, I draw (much as does Ludwig [2016b]) on an earlier Foucauldian notion of biopolitics as constitutively racist and, as such, exclusionary (Foucault 2004, 254–263). See also note 12 to this chapter.

normative in the sense that not only normation, but normalization too depends upon a division between 'normal' and 'abnormal' which is indeed dichotomous (contra Ludwig [2016b, 34] as well as Engel [2002]). However fluid the boundaries between 'normal' and 'abnormal' may have become in recent times, in line with Ludwig's expression of a 'continuum of normality' (2016b, 28): The term 'normal' cannot do without its Other, the term 'abnormal', by definition (cf. Hark 1999, 79–80). Towards the end of any 'continuum of normality' there remains an arbitrarily set boundary which differentiates it from the 'absolutely abnormal', and beyond which a pathologization of subjects continues to hold – of those subjects who do not count as optimizable or for whom no inclusion is intended. (This is evident, for instance, in the institutional practices of psychiatry and psychology which – in conjunction with the comprehensive therapeutization of society – continue to operate through 'asylums' with closed wards, where 'measures' such as physically tying up 'patients', and medicating them forcibly, are maintained [Thesing 2017].)

Link recognizes this at certain points (e.g. Link 2013, 9, 58–59, 112). But his characterization of normalism as essentially independent of normativity (Link 1998, 2013) contradicts this acknowledgment. This characterization is based on a static, dehistoricized (see Link 1998, 254) and very narrow notion of normativity which corresponds to Foucault's reduction of normativity to the operation of a law understood in terms of prohibition (see above). The claim made by both writers that normalization or normalism is non-normative covers over its exclusionary character. The dependency of the term 'normality' upon its counterpart, the term 'abnormal', makes the first term *constitutively normative* in a much wider sense which, at the same time, is elementary: in the sense, that is, that the duality 'normal/abnormal' has a value-laden, hierarchizing as well as prescriptive character.

Link's theory of normalism in my view wouldn't be invalidated if he took to heart the critically inclined insight into the constitutive implication of 'normality' in value-laden normativity. Rather, his theory would become coherent only by way of this move. For, in the absence of this insight, it is unclear how the pressure or drive towards (self-)normalization comes about which, according to Link (2013), is central both to protonormalism and to flexible normalism, as well as to the dynamic interaction between both variants of normalism. According to my thesis, this pressure is generated via the abjecting designation 'abnormal', which provides the incentive or motivation for the drive to 'normalize', in the first place (see below). Link seems to assume this himself at many points in his writings. However, his characterization of the construct 'normality' as non-normative is inconsequent in that it fails to match this assumption. This characterization is also politically uncritical, as it makes it impossible conceptually to take account of the constitutive part borne by the stigmatized 'abnormal' for the establishment of *any* normalism – even 'flexible normalism', which hence is by no means wholly flexible (in the sense that it would involve entirely permeable boundaries) but does have a repressive side.

The constitutive interlocking of the 'productive' side from which power today shows itself to *some* subjects predominantly – namely, in its constructionist modality – with the rigid, even repressive side from which *others* experience power (including neoliberal power) in large part has been taken account of theoretically in the most apposite way by Butler: From the abjective (Butler 1993, 3) designation 'abnormal' (or 'pathological'), implying as it does an injunction to differentiate from it (i.e. not to be identified with such a label), there results a movement of just such differentiation; a distancing movement – even as the latter is not performed with equal success by everyone. Along with the disciplining of 'abnormals', involving normation – with a view to gender, this affects particularly trans and inter persons by way of their continuing pathologization – (self-)normalization too, as engaged in by those who are (found to be) 'apt' and are permitted to do so, is therefore inherently normative in the sense in which Butler (1993) has analyzed normativity: namely, in the sense just described, of the *normalizing effect of abjection, i.e. its effect of approximating the latter subjects to the norm* (see also Tyler 2013).

Theorizing that severs the link between the 'flexible' and the 'rigid' faces of power whilst privileging its 'flexible' face analytically (flexible, that is, only for certain subjects) generates a dualistic rather than a relational perspective. Moreover, this perspective ironically is itself *normative* in that it is conceptually based and, hence, modeled upon the social location, living conditions, and experience of subjects who tend to be positioned hegemonically, rendering these *as the norm*. And in a naturalized form, i.e. without this step being critically reflected upon and thereby marked as such, in the first place.

To conceive of normativity – and, hence, of heteronormativity – as a purely juridical distinction between the permitted and the forbidden which, qua technology of power, operates negatively and which exists only in a single form – no matter whether in doing so one follows Foucault (2007, 56, 46, 5) or Link (2013) – is to obscure more subtle modes in which normativity operates. It is therefore counterproductive for political and social analyses which are queer-feminist and antiracist at the same time (cf. Mesquita 2012). In contrast, a Butlerian understanding of norms as existing exclusively in their citation and, thus, as subject to historical transformation – an iterative resignification (Butler 1993) – makes it possible to conceive of normativity as a dimension of discourses *as such*, in the sense that *any* discourse entails an evaluative and prescriptive dimension (whether explicitly or implicitly so) (see also chapter 5). As a principal dimension of the discursive, normativity frames technologies of power per se, in their multiplicity. Normativity is at work in different technologies of power *in historically differing modalities*.

Taking a Butlerian understanding of normativity as a point of departure, the relationship between normalization and normation qua intersecting technologies of power can be sketched as follows, drawing as well upon the insight of an *earlier* Foucault into the intrinsic normativity of any possible notion of 'normality' – which applies as well to any accumulation of statistical knowledge orienting, for instance, to 'normal distributions' that would profess to be 'purely descriptive' (as implied uncritically by the later Foucault as well as by Link [see above]). In *Discipline and Punish*, Foucault wrote with a view to quantifying – continuous rather than binary (1991, 180–184) – systems for the measurement of subjects' performance, which qua "'value-giving' measure" (Foucault 1991, 183) he regarded as essential to disciplinary power:

"And by the play of this quantification, this circulation of awards and debits, thanks to the continuous calculation of plus and minus points, the disciplinary apparatuses hierarchized the 'good' and the 'bad' subjects in relation to one another. Through this micro-economy of a perpetual penality operates *a differentiation that is not one of acts, but of individuals themselves, of their nature*, their potentialities, their level or *their value*. By assessing acts with precision, discipline judges individuals 'in truth'" (Foucault 1991, 181; emphasis added; see also Foucault 1991, 182–183).

Foucault added:

"The perpetual penality that traverses all points and supervises every instant in the disciplinary institutions compares, differentiates, hierarchizes, homogenizes, *excludes* [emphasis added]. In short, it *normalizes* [emphasis in the original]. [...] For the marks that once indicated status, privilege and affiliation were increasingly replaced – or at least supplemented – by a whole range of *degrees of normality* [emphasis added] indicating membership of a homogeneous social body but also playing a part in classification, hierarchization and the distribution of rank." (1991, 183–184)

Informed by these remarks, I posit with a view to the present that those subjected to technologies of normation continue to be defined *in terms of an essence, their (imputed) 'character'* (contra Engel 2009, 151) – contrary to (the later) Foucault's construction of neoliberalism as a grid of intelligibility in whose terms "[t]he criminal is nothing other than absolutely anyone whomsoever" (Foucault 2010, 253; emphasis added; see above). Today, the violent essentialization of the pathologized and excluded coexists with constructionist discourses revolving around optimization and a 'responsible' government of self (cf. Engel 2009, 151; von Osten 2003, 9; see also Villa 2008, 248, 250, 267). But the latter discourses – this must be emphasized – are available primarily to subjects who at least tend to be positioned hegemonically; that is, particularly to 'white' middle- to upper-class persons who are neither trans nor inter, and have been neither psychiatrized nor handicapped, whether physically or mentally. This discursive contrast seems to me to be definitive of discrimination today, whether it takes the form of (inter alia) racist or/and ableist practices. That is to say, this discursive contrast makes for the decisive difference between normation on the one hand and normalization on the other.

Conclusion

To conceptualize (hetero-)normativity and (hetero-)normalization as separate, (potentially) mutually independent technologies of power of which one has replaced the other entirely or at least as the main one is to risk rendering invisible, on the level of theory, the part played by those who do not count as 'suited for integration'. (Whether it be, for instance, trans persons of color, those unemployed long-term, or/and those subjected to psychiatric 'treatment'.) It is to risk reinforcing their subalternization even further. We need to take account more consistently, in producing theory and diagnosing the present, of the role of those affected by exclusion *as abjected subjects*[14] *from whom others seek to set themselves apart in the spirit of normalization.* This makes it necessary to frame their social abjection as *constitutive* of normalization; its constitutive outside (Butler 1993, esp. 3; contra Engel 2002, 228) and, thus, to clarify normalization's exclusiveness, of which Foucault failed to see that it marks not merely discipline, but also neoliberalism fundamentally. As a way of bringing into view the functionalization of 'abnormals' (see note 10) as 'Western' societies' constitutive outside in the present more vigorously – i.e. with greater theoretical and political consequence – I have proposed to theorize (hetero-)normalization and (hetero-)*normation* (not least of trans and inter persons) as a tandem of mutually intersecting technologies of power, which *qua*

---

14   Or, phrased more accurately, as those whose status as subjects is precisely being questioned/repudiated.

tandem is *normative in a Butlerian sense*. Specifically, in the sense that the constitution of self, and the neoliberal government, of hegemonic subjects (too) operates via an abjection of their essentialized Others: of those pathologized as 'abnormal'.

Postscript

Amir and Kotef (2018), whose reading of Foucault with a view to his distinction between 'normalization' and 'normation' comes closer to my own reading of Foucault than any other authors', have gone some way towards deconstructing the opposition which I criticize in Foucault, between a 'normalization' understood as purely descriptive or non-judgmental and 'normation' as its prescriptive counterpart. They do so in the specific context of their study of full-body scanners, used at airports, as a technology of power. The authors point out that this technology is designed to operate in a manner free of discrimination, in line with an understanding of 'normal' in the statistical sense of 'frequent', by the logic of which *infrequent* bodily features are identified as potential security threats. They identify this sense of 'normal' with Foucault's term 'normalization' as a technology of power *devoid of judgment*, i.e. in contrast with 'normation' as a technology of power understood as *involving norms* (see the extensive quotation from Amir/Kotef [2018] at the beginning of this chapter). However, as the authors argue: "While 'normal' in this context supposedly represents the mere prevalence of a given phenomenon, these [security, C.B.] systems ultimately reproduce categories which are very much aligned with social norms." (Amir/Kotef 2018, 237). They elaborate:

> "the objectively calculated normalization would *necessarily* replicate the categories of normation. This assertion rests on the claim that processes of empirical (statistical) normalization of the body, measuring human behaviour and constitution, are *irrefutably entangled* in the ways in which the body has been *disciplined* and categorized, deciphered and signified. This entanglement, queer

theory teaches us, is always already immersed in *normation* processes. *Bodies can be sorted, measured, compared and averaged* only after they have been normalized; *only after they have been construed by the categories that render bodies intelligible and are, thus, the effects of prior disciplinary processes* (Butler, 1993). At least when engaged in the particularities of bodies, then, the second type of normalization (that of biopolitics) [i.e. normalization in the strict sense as defined by Foucault, C.B.] unavoidably carries with it the first type (of discipline) [i.e. the type of normalization in a wider sense which Foucault calls 'normation', C.B.]. What we have here is a technological manifestation of Butler's structural claim that the liberal paradigm of inclusion can never achieve its promise: *there will always be forms of exclusion.* Even if such algorithms were designed under different sets of assumptions concerning the structure of gender categories, *abnormalities of some kind would necessarily still be produced* by these technologies and marked as a security problem (be it heart rate, body heat, size, mobility or functionality for instance). As we have argued, *without such a production, there would be no meaning to 'threat' within this paradigm.*" (2018, 249–250; emphasis added)

In other words, the very purpose of the full-body scanner, of identifying potential threats to security, is inscribed with the notion of the 'abnormal': "the logic of operation of the algorithm [based on which the full-body scanner functions, C.B.] is designed to identify threat with *deviation (from the 'normal' body or 'normal' human behaviour)*" (Amir/Kotef 2018, 249; emphasis added). Hence, "in such systems *without 'abnormalities' the concept of 'threat' loses its meaning.*" (Amir/Kotef 2018, 244; emphasis added)

Amir and Kotef in the above quotations come close to arguing, as I have done above, that the notion of the 'abnormal' is both constitutively devaluing (and, hence, far from being non-judgmental, involves norms) and constitutive of *any possible notion of 'normal'.* However, they confine their argument to the specific empirical case on which their study focuses, and to norms *pertaining to the body* which form its context. They stop short of actually advancing the argument that *any possible notion of 'normal'* is constitutively *normative* (in the sense of 'involving norms'). Instead of making this argument as a matter of theoretical principle (with Butler, whom they do cite; much as I have above), they actually validate the notion advanced by Foucault that there are two possible meanings of 'normal', only one of which is evaluative whereas the other is devoid of normative judgment. Thus, in the concluding section of their paper, they reiterate their view that:

> "the two meanings of 'normal' obtained by these two configurations of power [disciplinary power and biopower/security, C.B.] remain distinct. While one is a predefined and an ethically-loaded model that dictates judgement based on one's ability to conform to it, the other is a *purely empirical measurement*, extrapolated from the order of things." (Amir/Kotef 2018, 250; emphasis added)

Like Ludwig (2016b), Link (1998; 2013) and other writers mentioned in this chapter, Amir and Kotef thus ultimately take on board the Foucauldian notion that normalization ('in the strict sense') is non-normative in principle.[15] I have argued in this chapter that this theorem

---

15   More unambiguously than Amir and Kotef, Chambers (2017) seems to me to perpetuate a quasi-positivism that resonates with Foucault's own, even if it comes in a different terminological version than Foucault's. (As stated in note 3 to this chapter, Chambers defines Foucault's terms differently than does Foucault. This applies especially to the term 'normativity', the Foucauldian definition of which term Chambers simply omits.) Chambers for his part seeks to maintain a "distinction between the norm and the *dispositif* of power that upholds and enforces norms" (2017, 21), as if norms themselves could be situated outside power. Stating that "the norm is a distribution of cases, *a dispersion across the entire* [bell, C.B.] *curve*" (2017, 14; emphasis in the original), he actually argues that a "statistical distribution of sex and sexuality" – that is, presumably, of bodily features as much as of sexual practices, for instance – is not what "the critique of heteronormativity" opposes, and that to do so would be "naive" (2017, 21–22). "[I]t would be illogical to be against the basic idea that there is a norm around sexuality in the sense that there is a normal statistical distribution of sexual identities and practices" (2017, 23). In my view, to state this is to miss the Butlerian argument that there is no 'sex' before 'gender', that is, before or outside power (Butler 1990, 1993). The very technique

is uncritical and impedes an understanding of neoliberalism as being based on constitutive exclusions which pathologize and abject some of us as 'abnormal'.

---

of statistical measurement is always already inscribed with the normatively charged, hierarchizing, *discursive* notion of 'normal' vs. 'abnormal' – without which it would have no *raison d'être* – and, more generally, with 'the will to knowledge' (Foucault 1990). To define 'norms' in terms of a statistical 'normal distribution' understood as 'natural' and outside of power is in fact analogous to ontologizing 'sex' as prediscursive (cf. Bruining 2016; see also Amir/Kotef 2018, as quoted in the Postscript to this chapter). Chambers, however, seems to be doing as much when he writes:

"norms are more than averages; they are distributions. Normativity is more than a norm; it is a name for the power relations produced and sustained when a norm comes to *matter* within a particular social order (or subculture of that order). Normativity connotes, in a way that 'norm' by itself need not, a distribution understood to be – and often culturally and politically enforced as – proper, truthful, and/or *right*. This compulsive power of normativity can thereby render the tails of a normal curve as wrong, deviant, and/or pathological. Hence normativity can generate a polarity between the normal and the abnormal." (Chambers 2017, 22; emphasis in the original).

Contrary to these words, the thrust of my argument in this chapter has been that statistically measurable 'facts' are unintelligible in the absence of the hierarchical opposition 'normal/abnormal'. In this sense, statistically measurable 'facts' are discursively constituted. This does not mean that 'facts' – such as bodily features, for instance – are therefore not material, or *'nothing but* discourse' (Butler 1993, 2015b, 17–35). See chapter 2 in this book for further discussion.

5 Negativity/Affirmation
Moving Beyond Reverse Discourse, With – and
Partially Beyond – Sara Ahmed
Or: In Defense of Happiness

Introduction

Recent debates in queer as well as feminist theory have tended to
be structured by binary opposition: paranoid vs. reparative reading
(Cvetkovich 2012; Love 2007b; critically: Pedwell 2014; Stacey 2014),
for vs. against the 'antisocial thesis' (Edelman 2004; Caserio *et al.*
2006; Muñoz 2009), negativity vs. affirmation (Love 2007a, 2007b;
Halberstam 2011; Braidotti 2002). Thus, according to Joshua J. Weiner
and Damon Young:

> "The most prominent debates in queer theory of recent years have
> located the political promise of queerness in the espousal of one of
> two positions: one must be 'for' (a queer version of) the social or one
> must be, as queer, 'against' the social (as we know it). [...] Such a binary,
> we argue, presents a false choice" (2011, 224).

Similarly, Brigitte Bargetz observes, citing Anu Koivunen:

> "Within current queer feminist debates on affect, 'two camps'
> (Koivunen 2010, 23) have appeared to emerge. For Koivunen, there are
> 'at least implicitly and metaphorically' two 'new caricatures of feminist
> scholars': 'those for joy, those for melancholy; those for life, those for

death; those for reparative criticisms, those constrained by paranoia'." (2015, 583)

Some of those positioning themselves as embracing 'negativity' – such as Heather Love (2007a) and Jack (Judith) Halberstam (2011) – construe their position (which is left rather implicit) as if they believed it possible to embrace negativity without espousing affirmation precisely in virtue of doing so: as if embracing negativity meant only *opposing* an affirmation of anything, rather than, precisely, *affirming* negativity. Against such a self-misunderstanding, which fails to see or to acknowledge the paradox entailed in evaluating negativity positively, Sara Ahmed has argued (in the context of addressing the affect of shame):

"I am not sure how it is possible to embrace the negative without turning it into a positive. To say 'yes' to the 'no' is still a 'yes'. To embrace or affirm the experience of shame, for instance, sounds very much like taking a pride in one's shame – a conversion of bad feeling into good feeling" (2006, 175; see also Ahmed 2010, 162).

Pure negativity, in other words, is an impossibility. Yet the position Ahmed takes regarding the emotion of happiness is in tension with this insight. Her treatment of the subject of happiness is riven with tension, as I aim to show in this chapter. In much of *The Promise of Happiness* (Ahmed 2010), Ahmed rejects happiness per se, for the most part without acknowledging that – as I wish to argue – this is, likewise, an impossibility. I propose that Ahmed does not take to heart the consequences of the insight that it is impossible to desire 'bad feeling' without converting it into 'good feeling' when this insight is applied to happiness and its negation, unhappiness: Effectively, her principal argument in *The Promise of Happiness* engages in a reverse discourse that promotes unhappiness as desirable or positive, yet without seeing that this is effectively to code it as the *happier* condition, or at least as a more positive state. In contrast, I argue that when happiness is understood (as it should be) as *being affected positively*, then desiring happiness is inescapable. As we shall see, much in Ahmed's writing on happiness bears out this point. Yet her account remains contradictory in failing fully to acknowledge it. I believe that resolving this contradiction will advance critical discourse. What is needed, I argue, is not a blanket rejection of happiness as such, but an alternative, counter-hegemonic *framing* of what it might mean to be affected positively. Reclaiming the desire to be so affected – in other words, reclaiming happiness – is the theoretically more consequent lesson to be drawn from Ahmed's highly convincing political critique of the ways in which this term is framed *hegemonically*. We should not surrender happiness, and an appraisal of happiness as what is good, to hegemonic discourse – as she sets out to do (2010, 62).

But what is at stake in debating this issue is much more than Ahmed's line of theorizing happiness, in particular. By way of close-reading *The Promise of Happiness*, I wish to question the fundamental queer-theoretical consensus to the effect that queer theory is antinormative (Jagose 2015; Wiegman/Wilson 2015) or that 'the normative' exists only 'out there' in the hegemonic other (e.g., in "heteropatriarchy" [Ferguson 2004, 26–27, 29]). More than this, I question the very possibility of escaping normativity. The very term 'antinormative' is a contradiction in terms to the extent that to oppose normativity is itself a normatively charged act, if by 'normativity' we understand (as we should) any act that entails an evaluation, i.e., that assigns value. If queer theory is to live up to its self-imputed politicized character, then it needs to let go of the notion that it is normatively innocent. There is no such innocence – only competing styles of normativity. In what follows, I will work out what distinguishes hegemonic normative styles from an alternative style that is non-normalizing, based on Ahmed's analysis of happiness. Much as her analysis is riven with contradiction, it encompasses a normative style which I characterize as egalitarian and denaturalizing (and, as such, as power-cognizant rather than power-evasive [cf. Frankenberg 1993]). I argue that practicing a normative style that is self-avowedly implicated in power is politically more critical and theoretically more self-reflexive than styling one's own (queer-theoretical) position as being free of normativity. It is ultimately more in keeping with one of Michel Foucault's central insights, contrary to a received reading of Foucault (Lemke 2007, 67–68) – and even with Friedrich Nietzsche's affirmation of the will to power. Scholarly writing that is unaware of being implicated in normativity risks being complicit more readily in hegemonic forms of normativity, which I characterize as unegalitarian and reifying (cf. Schotten 2019). Those are necessary ingredients of a *normalizing* normativity, which I critique as much as other queer feminist theorists do.

My disagreement with much queer theorizing, then, does not concern its substance – characterized in terms of "anti-morality" by C. Heike Schotten (2019, title) – so much as its self-understanding (the way in which its substance is framed at the metalevel), which I consider to be mistaken. This results, as I conclude, in a politically uncritical construction of 'queer (theory)' as being less implicated than it really is in what it contests. With Foucault, I want to insist that there is no outside to power.

Since my analysis owes much to Ahmed's work, particularly to *The Promise of Happiness*, I want to acknowledge at the outset how enriching I find her work to be as well as the large extent to which I agree with some aspects of her analysis of happiness, from which I have learned a great deal – much as I find its overall direction to be misguided.

In what follows, I first summarize Ahmed's critique of hegemonic framings of happiness. I then outline in what ways her rejection of happiness per se contradicts the implications of this critique, and is unconvincing in virtue of engaging a reverse discourse. In the next, lengthiest part of this chapter, I analyze these two main strands of the argument comprising Ahmed's account of happiness, in terms of mutually conflicting normative styles – one of them mimicking a hegemonic normative style that is unegalitarian and reifying, and the other exemplifying an alternative normative style which is egalitarian and denaturalizes normativity. Queer theory is always already normative – at its best, in just such an alternative form. Applied to happiness, I conclude, this form can be truly egalitarian only when it is non-dualistic, refusing to play happiness and unhappiness against each other in virtue of refusing to dismiss *either* of these emotions, whether it be unhappiness (as in hegemonic discourse) *or happiness* (as rejected per se in parts of Ahmed's discourse). A counter-hegemonic normative style is receptive to both of these affects, whilst emphasizing their potential contiguity.

Ahmed's critique of hegemonic framings of happiness

The Promise of Happiness offers a highly perceptive analysis of a number of ways of invoking happiness that reinforce inequality and domination. Happiness is socially *distributed*, Ahmed argues (2010, 162): happiness for some occurs at the cost of others' unhappiness. Thus, for instance, she writes with reference to Ursula Le Guin's (1987) short story "The Ones Who Walk Away from Omelas": "We recognize how much the promise of happiness depends upon the localization of suffering; others suffer so that a certain 'we' can hold on to the good life." (2010, 195). This occurs in part in virtue of what Ahmed calls a "happiness duty" (e.g., 2010, 59): Some subjects oblige others to pursue happiness by way of pursuing particular goals, or attaining particular things ("happy objects" [2010, 20–49, 54]). "[I]f you have this or have that, if you do this or do that, then happiness is what follows", as Ahmed (2010, 29) phrases what thus amounts to a promise of happiness held out as reward for orienting towards the 'right' goals or things (2010, 45, 54, 129). In this way, pursuing happiness assumes the function of a social prescription of conformity with *hegemonic* norms, in particular. More than that, the "happiness duty" is invoked according to Ahmed as a duty to be pursued so as to make *others* happy:

> "unhappy people are represented [in positive psychology, here: by the author Michael Argyle, C.B.] as deprived, as unsociable and neurotic [...]. Individuals must become happier for others: positive psychology describes this project as not so much a right as a responsibility. We have a responsibility for our own happiness insofar as promoting our own happiness is what enables us to increase other people's happiness." (Ahmed 2010, 9)

So unhappiness is constructed as a state to be avoided, not (ultimately) for the sake of those potentially affected by it, but rather for the sake of those thus wishing to be made comfortable by way of imposing a happiness duty on others – that is, by way of pressurizing others into social conformity (2010, 58, 158): *I am (un-)happy if you are (un-)happy* (2010, 91).

It is not difficult to recognize in this framing of happiness modes of dominating others that pursue the happiness of some at the expense of others – and not contingently, but with a normalizing thrust: Not to conform, for instance, to heteronormativity is here minimally *implied* to be a recipe for unhappiness, and those who will not or cannot conform are thus likely both to be *made* unhappy by such normalizing discourse, and possibly to *prefer* being unhappy, *if 'happiness' is identified with just such normalization*.

Throwing the baby out with the bathwater: Ahmed's reverse discourse

Against happiness?

This seems, in fact, to be the ground based on which much of the argument comprising *The Promise of Happiness* – but not all lines of argument pursued in this work – reject(s) happiness *as such* in favor of being unhappy (as against merely rejecting a specifically hegemonic framing of happiness, as characterized above). Ahmed writes, for instance:

> "Imagination is what makes women look beyond the script of happiness to a different fate. [...] Feminist readers might want to challenge this association between unhappiness and female imagination, which in the moral economy of happiness, makes female imagination a bad thing. But if we do not operate in this economy – that is, *if we do not assume that happiness is what is good* – then we can read the link between female imagination and unhappiness

differently. We might explore how imagination is what allows women to be liberated from happiness and the narrowness of its horizons. We might want the girls to read the books that enable them to be overwhelmed with grief." (2010, 62; emphasis added)

"I do not want to offer an alternative definition of happiness (a good happiness that can be rescued from bad happiness), as this would keep in place the very idea that happiness is what we should promote." (2010, 217)

"If to challenge the right to happiness is to deviate from the straight path, then political movements involve sharing deviation with others. There is joy, wonder, hope, and love in sharing deviation. If to share deviation is to share what causes unhappiness, even joy, wonder, hope, and love are ways of *living with* rather than *living without* unhappiness." (2010, 196; emphasis in the original)

But this position – rejecting happiness per se, rather than merely specific discursive framings, or modes of understanding 'happiness' (see also Ahmed 2010, 2, 77–79, 192–193) – cannot be sustained except at the cost of self-contradiction. What, after all, could be the ground of Ahmed's critique of the uneven distribution of happiness which must necessarily result from its hegemonic construction as outlined above, if not the view that it is *unjust* to deny true happiness to some (whatever this might mean to them) – as she implies herself at one point (Ahmed 2010, 63)? Or, put the other way round, how to critique the unequal distribution of unhappiness other than on the grounds that it is *unjust* for some to be (made) unhappy in ways that relate systematically to social inequality and normalization – as she implies herself at another point (Ahmed 2010, 194)? To formulate this critique is, at least implicitly, to frame unhappiness as undesirable or uncomfortable to those affected by it – and, thus, is to cede the very point which Ahmed explicitly disputes: that unhappiness is undesirable. In turn, this point entails that happiness is preferable to feeling unhappy, let alone to pronounced suffering. Thus, as Elizabeth Stephens characterizes one aspect of Ahmed's critique of the unequal social distribution of happiness:

> "a key point of Ahmed's argument is that happiness is a political condition rather than a personal state. We see this in the way happiness is unequally distributed amongst social groups and individuals, disproportionately experienced by those subjects who occupy privileged cultural positions. As a result, Ahmed argues: 'The face of happiness looks rather like the face of privilege'" (Stephens 2015, 278).

Clearly, the latter statement (by Ahmed, as cited by Stephens) implies that experiencing happiness is to experience an advantage over and against those who are denied this experience.

Beyond dualism

Perhaps what is needed is a more differentiated view of un-/happiness than one that would either reject or affirm unhappy affective states without qualification. This becomes apparent particularly when we juxtapose Ahmed's rejection of happiness with Rosi Braidotti's affirmative feminism, which Ahmed critiques for its inverse rejection of bleakness in favor of positive affects (2010, 87). Stephens reconstructs Ahmed's general critique as follows:

> "To avoid sadness, as Braidotti encourages us to do, is to ignore the plight of those who are excluded from happiness, and to transform political oppression into a personal failure to overcome that negativity. Compulsory happiness and positivity is thus for some an additional source of suffering and sadness" (2015, 277).

This critique presupposes an evaluation of suffering and sadness as uncomfortable and (therefore) undesirable states for those affected by them, as we have seen. Yet, according to Ahmed, *it is precisely an attitude of rejection of such negative feelings that contributes to the unequal social distribution of emotions* whereby some are privileged to experience positive feelings while others are in large part excluded from that experience. Her critique of affirmative feminism thus would seem to be that it is precisely an unqualified rejection of negative feelings that results in affective social inequality. It is, in other words, an *egalitarian* critique whose implicit normative thrust consists in the claim that it would be desirable for happiness to be accessible to all.

Obviously, this claim starkly contradicts the principal argument of the *Promise of Happiness* to the effect that to assume that happiness is what is good is to operate within the moral economy of happiness (see above; see also Ahmed 2010, 2, 13, 14, 77–79, 192–193). I posit that this contradiction is symptomatic of the impossibility of rejecting happiness wholeheartedly, or of desiring unhappiness wholeheartedly, without ambiguity or a qualifying 'but'. This is precisely because the identification of happiness, understood in the broad sense of being affected positively or benignly, with "what is good" (Ahmed, see above) is inescapable. To seek to dispute it must *necessarily* result in self-contradiction. This is what accounts for the contradictory character of the various, mutually conflicting arguments and normative styles comprising *The Promise of Happiness*: Apart from the implication of her egalitarian critique of affective social inequality, as demonstrated above – namely, that unhappiness is ultimately *un*desirable, contrary to Ahmed's explicit approach of rejecting happiness, and affirming unhappiness – she also contradicts that approach in that at times she *does* affirm positive affects as "what is good". She does so sometimes in the shape of using other terms that signify positive affects, beside the term 'happiness', while explicitly affirming this alternative as desirable. Thus she invokes "joy" as an alternative positive affect (e.g. 2010, 69). At other times, Ahmed even uses the term 'happiness' *itself* affirmatively (i.e. as something desirable, to be appreciated, to be wished for), thereby directly subverting her explicit approach of rejecting happiness as such (as against merely rejecting specific, hegemonic framings of the term). For instance, contrary to this explicit approach ("if anything I write from a position of skeptical disbelief in happiness as a technique for living well" [2010, 2]), she clearly does offer an alternative, affirmative framing of 'happiness' – as I am arguing that we should – when sketching what she refers to as "a revolutionary happiness" (2010,

198; see also Ahmed 2010, 103, 115–120). She even invokes alternative "happy object[s]" (2010, 115) despite her critical notion of such objects (2010, 198). These inconsistencies, too, are symptomatic of the fact that an approach of rejecting happiness *tout court* is unsustainable. Much in our discourse, including Ahmed's theoretical discourse, becomes unintelligible, incomprehensible, if we try to pursue this approach, since we cannot help but affirm 'happiness' if this term is understood as I propose we should understand it (see below), namely, in the general sense of 'being affected positively'. I submit that when we seem to reject happiness as such, it is really *particular notions* of happiness that we reject. (We might call our alternative, affirmative account of 'being affected positively' differently – e.g., 'joy' as an alternative to 'happiness' – or we might not. My own preference is to reappropriate the term 'happiness' for contestatory purposes rather than cede the terrain to hegemonic discourse.)

Ultimately, what I wish to critique about Ahmed's theorization of happiness is that it engages in a reverse discourse to Braidotti's, and to hegemonic constructions of happiness, in virtue of trying to reject happiness (without succeeding at it) as completely as those competing discourses reject unhappiness. In keeping with the recent debates in queer theory addressed at the beginning of this chapter, it is as if we could only be 'for' or 'against' happiness and, correspondingly, 'against' or 'for' its opposite. It is as if, with such a binary positing of the options available, it becomes impossible to qualify unhappiness *as a way of being affected negatively* which, while producing discomfort and potentially even extreme degrees of suffering, *is still to be accepted, and even opened up to*, because to reject negative emotional states will result in a biopolitical abjection and exclusion of those affected (the most) by such states – as indicated above in Stephens' words. The rationale here would be that negative states such as unhappiness and suffering cannot be wished away at will, and thus need to be accepted and attended to, without being applauded. This orientation towards negative affects entails *both* affirmation (of their reality) and negation (a recognition of the potential for severe suffering entailed in them, and thus, of the desire to escape such suffering). As such, it entails a constitution of negative affects, such as sadness, as *both undesirable and unavoidable*.

Conversely, rather than attempting to maintain a blanket rejection of happiness, which cannot be sustained, as I have argued, happiness might simultaneously be affirmed as a desirable state and *critiqued to the extent that it is framed in hegemonic ways* that are oppressive to some of us (thus actually generating *un*happiness). I propose that this is a more coherent and a more differentiated approach to being affected positively than Ahmed's unqualified rejection of happiness as such. This approach acknowledges the impossibility of rejecting happiness (as 'being affected positively') wholeheartedly, and the ambiguity of embracing unhappiness (as 'being affected negatively'), which turns the negative into a positive (Ahmed 2006, 175; see above), thereby implicitly construing it as the ultimately *happier* or better state – in keeping with Ahmed's own insight concerning the affect of shame (formulated in another work), as cited above. In *Promise*, Ahmed does at one point acknowledge, in agreement with Michael D. Snediker (2009), that "queer affirmations of negativity are not simply negative. To embrace the negative or to say yes to a no cannot be described as a purely negative gesture. To affirm negation is still an affirmation" (Ahmed 2010, 162). But in this book as a whole, as an approach to un-/happiness, Ahmed fails to heed this very lesson. I will say more on how I conceive of the relationship between (un-)happiness as an affect and normativity (negativity vs. affirmation) further below.

To desire (political) change for the better *is* to desire greater happiness

Significantly, in some parts of *The Promise of Happiness*, Ahmed focuses on suffering rather than on more moderate states of unhappiness. In Chapter 2, entitled "Feminist Killjoys", she states in the general context of discussing (mere) unhappiness (e.g., 2010, 70) – in which context she casts "feminist consciousness as a form of unhappiness" (2010, 53) that she codes as constructive, as indicating "the limitations of happiness as a horizon of experience" (2010, 53) – that "[w]e could describe happiness quite simply as a convention" (2010, 64). I consider this to be a rather un-affective characterization which fails to empathize with those excluded from happiness. But this is different elsewhere in the book, where Ahmed speaks, more dramatically, of (for instance) "misery" and "suffering" rather than only of "unhappiness" (2010, 195). Here, she emphasizes precisely the need for a willingness to open up to unhappiness and the unhappy rather than maintain an indifference towards them – in accordance with what, above, I have characterized as an egalitarian critique on Ahmed's part of affective social inequality. In line with such a more empathetic stance, Ahmed sometimes acknowledges that actually to *suffer* (rather than merely to be unhappy) is to desire to escape, or at least to reduce the intensity, of one's suffering (see, e.g., 2010, 114, 120). I feel that not to recognize this point would be to disavow how unbearable suffering, physical or otherwise, can be. Giving up on happiness (2010, 64) may seem to be possible and desirable more readily when the alternative is taken to be mere unhappiness than when what is at issue is severe suffering. Therefore, such a project may well risk giving up on those whose lives barely feel worth living, if at all. It may, in other words, entail the very indifference to the *most* unhappy which Ahmed critiques. It may be a project unaffordable to those who suffer to an extreme extent.

Without a recognition of the link between suffering and the desire for change – change, specifically, for the better – political struggle would in fact be unintelligible; it wouldn't make any sense (see also chapter 3 of this book). This point, too, is implicitly acknowledged by Ahmed when she writes with reference to the novel, *The Well of Loneliness* by Radclyffe Hall (1982), that the suffering depicted therein could stir in queers a desire for revolution:

"Not only does the novel explain the unhappiness of its ending as an effect of the violence of the happiness that resides within the straight world but it locates the promise of happiness for queers in revolution against the structures – the walls – that keep that world in place." (2010, 103)

A desire for revolution, as political desire for change, would be unintelligible, devoid of sense, if we did not acknowledge (whether explicitly or without avowing our acknowledgment) that suffering makes sentient beings want to escape it; to escape the sense of acute discomfort that suffering entails. But this *is*, at least implicitly, to affirm happiness as "what is good", contrary to the argument which Ahmed presents as the main thesis of her book: What do we strive towards if we strive to reduce suffering, if not for something *better* and (in that sense) towards at least *greater* happiness, in the sense of at least a certain affective improvement? Symptomatically, Ahmed in the above quotation connotes the "promise of happiness" – and thus, happiness itself – positively, contrary to her rejection of happiness at other points in her book of the same title. This is in tension with her statement, cited above, that: "We recognize how much the promise of happiness depends upon the localization of suffering; others suffer so that a certain 'we' can hold on to the good life." (2010, 195). In the previous quotation, Ahmed clearly offers an alternative framing of happiness and even of the promise of happiness – much as elsewhere in the book she rejects such a political project, as we have seen.

Even to affirm political hope – as Ahmed appears to do (2010, 160–198) – is indirectly to affirm happiness as "what is good", for what is hope if it is not hope for greater happiness to be attained in the future; for a better condition to be ahead? Ahmed disputes that such desire is necessarily entailed in hope – which, instead, she casts as ideally an affirmation of possibility without any particular content (e.g. 2010, 197, 218–219). But if hope does not necessarily entail a desire for a *better* future, then why bother to engage in political struggle, in the first place? I submit that to seek to escape suffering entails an evaluation of it as negative, and by the same token entails an appraisal of happiness – understood as the antithesis of suffering – as positive and, as such, desirable. Political struggle, and indeed any kind of struggle for change, is ultimately impossible without a desire for happiness.

It is impossible, then, to renounce that desire and the positive evaluation of happiness which is entailed in that desire. We can only avow such desire and the corresponding evaluation of happiness as good, or disclaim it. Conversely, it is impossible fully to embrace negative affective states, especially when they approach intense and continuous suffering, without acknowledging at least implicitly that it can verge on the unbearable to be affected by them; that this is *bad* – in the sense of making some lives unlivable. (Except in the case of masochism, which can be construed as an attainment of happiness by recourse to pain. In this case, *pain* is coded, and experienced, as affecting the subject positively.)

Queer normativity as an alternative normative style: Reframing happiness

Towards an egalitarian, denaturalizing normative style

So, what is my positive proposition with a view to framings of happiness that do not buttress hegemonic norms and existing social inequalities? I argue essentially that to construct happiness as something to be rejected per se is to remain stuck in a reverse discourse; in an oppositional mode that adheres to the 'anti' and, in virtue of doing so, adheres to binary opposition rather than questioning dualism as such: It is to accept the binary scheme of 'being either for or against' as the underlying conceptual model of the debate, including one's own position. This is to narrow one's vision as to the field of possible orientations concerning happiness and unhappiness to only two options. Above I have proposed a possible path that would open up this field of vision by way of sketching an orientation to happiness and unhappiness in which negation and affirmation are entangled rather than split apart into an either/or-ism: Specifically, I have argued that unhappiness is both unavoidable and undesirable; both to be accepted as a given (as an emotion it exceeds conscious control [Braunmühl 2012b]) and acknowledged to be a *negative* state, which it is impossible to embrace without qualification – especially when it takes the form of extreme suffering. I now want to propose that this alternative orientation to unhappiness amounts to a *normative style* of its own, one that diverges in politically significant ways from the kinds of hegemonic framing of unhappiness and happiness analyzed so compellingly by Ahmed. It is to the two main – mutually conflicting – argumentative strands discernible in her various specific analyses pertaining to these terms that I turn as a basis for explicating what most decisively differentiates normative styles of framing happiness that are, as I argue, politically objectionable from those that are politically constructive. I qualify as politically objectionable, hegemonic framings of happiness *accounts which reinscribe social inequality whilst naturalizing that very effect*. I evaluate as instantiating an alternative, truly counter-hegemonic normative style of framing happiness those moments in Ahmed's account of happiness in which she critiques framings of it that are *unegalitarian* and *reifying*. As I argue, this qualifies the normative style pursued by Ahmed herself in those moments as egalitarian as well as denaturalizing.

Before going into the details of this analysis, I want to make explicit what understanding of happiness and unhappiness I am operating with (as already alluded earlier). I understand happiness in the broad terms of 'what affects a subject positively' and unhappiness in terms of 'what affects a subject negatively'.[1] Such a broad understanding of happiness is important because, firstly, it can encompass many more specific framings of the term, including hegemonic and counter-hegemonic ones. Secondly, while this definition can appear to make tautological my claim that happiness is something one cannot not want (to borrow a formulation from Gayatri Chakravorty Spivak [1994, 285]) – after all, if happiness is what affects you positively, then 'of course' it is desirable for everyone – committing to this definition assumes specific importance in the context of Ahmed's work because it helps sort out a lack of clarity, even a certain amount of confusion, which shapes her analysis of happiness in my view: At times, Ahmed implies (as we have seen) that it is in such a broad sense that she rejects happiness, and refuses

---

1   This characterization has obvious resonances with Benedict (Baruch) de Spinoza's philosophy (2018), but I do not wish to take on board other aspects of the latter.

the notion of it as desirable, endorsing unhappiness as a preferred alternative – a position that is unsustainable, as argued earlier. At other times, Ahmed's rejection seems to be targeted more specifically at the *hegemonic* account of happiness which she reconstructs in her book (as briefly sketched above). In such moments of her analysis, she designates a preference either for alternative terms for 'being affected positively' – in particular, 'joy' – or even uses the term 'happiness' affirmatively (see above). This is to imply the very opposite of the first analytic move: namely, that happiness is indeed "what is good". So, *The Promise of Happiness* is starkly self-contradictory in that at times it endorses happiness or joy as a good (i.e., feelings that affect a subject positively by my definition), and at times rejects such endorsement as operating within the moral economy of happiness (2010, 62; see above), i.e. as itself being a hegemonic move. Since Ahmed refuses to offer a definition of happiness (2010, 217; see above), the contradiction does not necessarily surface as clearly as it could. (By contrast, the 'macro-definition' of happiness I have offered above helps bring the contradiction into focus.) But this leaves her entire analysis unclear. Her book thus conflates two alternative objects of critique: happiness per se (however understood) vs. happiness as framed in specific (especially hegemonic) discourses. The confused character of the analysis results from the fact that Ahmed does not distinguish these two very different objects of critique at all. Instead, she extrapolates from a critique of happiness *as framed hegemonically* to a rejection of happiness *as such*, as if the one clearly followed from the other – when it doesn't. So, her rationale for doing so remains obscure: Ahmed never justifies this move. (For instance, when she writes: "Happiness involves a form of orientation: the very hope for happiness means that we get directed in specific ways, as happiness is assumed to follow from some life choices and not others." [2010, 54]. Ahmed here too closely identifies striving for happiness with the particular '(happy) objects' it is hegemonically being tied to.) While this unaccounted-for leap renders her analysis intellectually somewhat unsatisfactory in my view, I think that it is all the more rewarding, as a way of clarifying what is at stake, to differentiate between these two main (mutually incompatible) strands of Ahmed's account in order to determine their very different political trajectories. That will be one task to be pursued in the remainder of this chapter. My position that we require alternative framings of 'being affected positively' to a hegemonic framing of happiness is in line with the *first* strand of Ahmed's argument, as just recapitulated: It is in line with the nature of her critique specifically of the *hegemonic* account of happiness as summarized above.

The inescapability of normativity

To understand happiness as what affects a subject positively is to understand affect and normativity to be mutually implicating: feelings entail an evaluation of how a given state of affairs affects *me* (cf. Hochschild 2003, 230–232). This is also implied by the very notion of 'positive' and 'negative' affects, of course, as commented upon by Bargetz (2015) and Koivunen (2010), for instance (see above). Conversely, I would argue that happiness and unhappiness are affective dimensions of normativity: evaluations of something as good or bad (for me). Normativity is *felt*, and as such, is an inescapable aspect of sensing and thinking the world.

With this view, I feel that I am upsetting what might be termed a queer-theoretical, counter-hegemonic consensus: The view that it is possible to produce discourse (e.g. theory) *without* being normative. This consensus comes in several variants: the notion of queer theory's *anti*normativity, which Annamarie Jagose (2015) has shown to be extremely widespread among queer theorists, or (as an alternative term to seemingly similar effect), that it is possible to produce discourse that is "nonnormative" (Ferguson 2004, 14, 144, 148). Jagose argues:

> "Queer theory's antinormativity, we can say, is evident in its anti-assimilationist, anticommunitarian or antisocial, anti-identitarian, antiseparatist, and antiteleological impulses. While each of these terms indexes lively archives of sharp and sometimes unresolved discussion rather than points of critical consensus, what is notable is the extent to which the legitimacy and foundational rightness of

different – sometimes even oppositional – positions are clinched via claims to antinormativity, a value that is thus universally acknowledged as the unimpeachable criterion for determining the queerness of any political stance or strategy." (2015, 27)

When I take issue with the queer-theoretical tenet that there is an outside to normativity (Wiegman/Wilson 2015) by insisting that it is impossible to escape the latter, it is important that we be clear as to what I do and do not mean by this. My understanding of normativity has nothing to do with Jürgen Habermas' position, that is to say, with any notion of transcendental norms understood as necessary 'foundations' that legislate an 'ought' which is presumed to be universally valid and binding on all (cf. Butler 1992, 6–8, 20, n. 4). Nor do I mean by 'normativity' what is meant by this term in much queer theory, namely, a *normalizing* discourse that distinguishes, for instance, between 'normal' and 'perverse' or 'pathological' (Wiegman/Wilson 2015; Jagose 2015; Berlant/Warner 1998). One of my central points is that *this is not the only form of normativity there is* (contra Wiegman/Wilson 2015). Normativity is to be understood in terms of *any practice or doing that has an evaluative dimension*. Queer discourse is not politically innocent of encoding values and, as such, hierarchies. It is, in this sense, implicated in what Foucault designated as an inextricable relationship between power and knowledge, or "truth and power" (1980). Contrary to readings of Foucault which assume that he was only interested in producing genealogies of how normative discourses have come into being and how they operate, as if this meant not being implicated, *oneself*, in a normative discourse in the sense which I wish to give this term (see, e.g., Lemke 2007, 67–68), I want to insist that the most consequent lesson to be derived from Foucault's dictum that there is no knowledge or discourse outside power is to recognize that this applies to *everyone's* knowledge production, including one's own. And that, moreover, being implicated in power relations and dynamics includes being implicated in one of the central mechanisms Foucault has shown power to operate by (and which queer theorists are so fond of emphasizing [Jagose 2015, 27, 31]): in normative discourse.

But this is not the end of the story: I am not saying that everyone, including queer theorists, is complicit in the production of a *normalizing* normativity.[2] Yet we are more likely unwittingly to be so complicit if we do not realize that there is a normative dimension to our own discourse, and in what particular ways it is normative. This is why I propose that it would be politically productive to work with the notion of *competing normative styles*, which may but need not be normalizing. This can assist us in cultivating an awareness of exactly how we participate in normativity. What I want to question, then, is the notion that there can be such a thing as a *value-free* – and, as such, a non-hierarchizing – discourse. Such a notion would be thoroughly un-Foucauldian. It would be highly depoliticizing. This is why it is of consequence how we use the term, 'normativity': *if we restrict it to hegemonic, normalizing styles of normativity*, as is common in queer theory (see above), *then we perpetuate the power-charged myth of a value-free, non-hierarchizing discourse, in terms of which we implicitly frame our own, alternative position.*

Just as I have argued that there is no outside to 'desiring happiness', so I am now arguing that there is no outside to normativity. Since 'happiness' on the view I am defending here *is* the feeling that associates with the evaluation of something as 'good', both points are connected: Subjects cannot *not* evaluate, and subjects cannot not *want* at an affective level what they evaluate as good. Conversely, merely in feeling

---

2   While Robyn Wiegman and Elizabeth A. Wilson (2015), too, state that (contrary to much queer theory) there is no outside to the normative, they implicitly treat normalization – i.e., a hegemonic form of normativity – as the only form of normativity there is. By contrast, I am concerned to show that normativity can take other, counter-hegemonic and politically constructive forms. (While Wiegman and Wilson view norms as *productive*, they question the possibility of a political alternative to normalization and do not allow for what I am referring to as a politically *constructive* – in the sense of 'counter-hegemonic' – mode of normativity.) For an in-depth discussion of the notions of normalization and normativity in their complexities, mutual relationship, and 'productive' vs. 'negative' dimensions, which considers in detail the changing usage of these terms by Foucault as well as their highly discrepant forms of usage 'post-Foucault', see chapter 4 and the Introduction to this book.

happy or closer to unhappiness, we engage normativity; we evaluate a situation or object.

The normative character of Ahmed's discourse

Contrary to what Ahmed presupposes in her Editorial to a *New Formations* special issue on "Happiness" (Ahmed 2007), her own discourse is very clearly normative. Like other queer theorists, Ahmed presumes that it is possible to stand outside normativity, and that standing outside normativity is characteristic of Cultural Studies approaches to happiness. This presumption is entailed in part in the following passages from the Editorial, entitled "The Happiness Turn":

> "Critiques of the happiness industry that call for a return to classical concepts of virtue not only sustain the association between happiness and the good, but also *suggest that some forms of happiness are better than others*. This distinction between a strong and weak conception of happiness *is clearly a moral distinction*: some forms of happiness are read as worth more than other forms of happiness, because they require more time and labour. Noticeably, within classical models, the forms of happiness that are higher are linked to the mind, and those that are lower are linked to the body. [...] *Hierarchies of happiness may correspond to social hierarchies that are already given*." (2007, 11; emphasis added)

Ahmed then juxtaposes a Cultural Studies approach to happiness to the above, as an alternative to it, and states:

> "Cultural Studies might in its very worldly orientation, offer a rigorous analysis of happiness and power: ideas of happiness support concepts of the good life that take the shape of some lives and not others. Reading happiness is a matter of reading how happiness and unhappiness are distributed and located within certain bodies and groups." (2007, 11)

The two kinds of approach are juxtaposed by Ahmed *as alternatives* – as if a Cultural Studies approach as envisaged by Ahmed did *not* "*suggest that some forms of happiness are better than others"* (see the previous quotation above). This involves picturing Cultural Studies in much the way Foucauldian genealogy is commonly understood, namely, as outlining (histories of) normative discourses and practices as if this entailed the possibility of abstaining from a normative perspective oneself, qua analyst (see above). As I have already argued, such abstinence is impossible. Ahmed is, in the above quotations, disavowing the normative character of her own 'take' on happiness. Yet its normative character is clear even in the above quotations themselves, which imply that a Cultural Studies perspective upon happiness is *better* than classical concepts of virtue. In her book, *The Promise of Happiness*, moreover, Ahmed at times (and at the end of the book) very clearly offers an alternative framing of 'happiness' that she presents as *better* than hegemonic or conventional framings of the term. Thus, the book ends in part on the following note, which is a comment on the film *Happy-Go-Lucky* (2008) by Mike Leigh:

> "In coming to value that which is not valued, and in finding joy in places that are not deemed worthy, we learn about the costs of value and worth. The happy-go-lucky character might seem unweighed by duty and responsibility; she might seem light as a feather. She might seem careless and carefree. But freedom from care is also a freedom to care, to respond to the world, to what comes up, *without defending oneself or one's happiness against what comes up."* (2010, 222; emphasis added)

This statement postulates an alternative value hierarchy (a distinction between better and worse forms of happiness) which, as such, is clearly normative. Yet, unlike the notions of happiness critiqued by Ahmed – both classical ones and those found in the "happiness industry" (see above: Ahmed 2007, 11) – Ahmed in the above quotations is promoting an *egalitarian* notion of happiness: *"Hierarchies of happiness may correspond to social hierarchies that are already given"*, as she observes in a critical vein. As against hierarchies of happiness that thus reinforce existing social inequalities, Ahmed proposes *valuing that which is not valued*, not *deemed worthy*. Her account (here as elsewhere) renders explicit the act of assigning value, and denaturalizes what is being naturalized or reified in hegemonic accounts of happiness, which Ahmed refers to as making "*a moral distinction* [in which, C.B.] some forms of happiness are read as worth more than other forms of happiness" (2007, 11; emphasis added; see above). Throughout her critiques of conventional, unegalitarian accounts of happiness, Ahmed analyzes how value within them is coded as *inhering in things* (e.g., in "happy objects"; see above) or *in subjects* (see also Ahmed 2010, 33–34, 37). Thus, in "The Happiness Turn", she writes:

> "Rather than assuming happiness is simply found in 'happy persons,' we can consider how claims to happiness make certain forms of personhood valuable. Attributions of happiness might be how social norms and ideals become affective, as if relative proximity to those norms and ideals creates happiness." (2007, 10)

In contrast, Ahmed's own account often – though not throughout – assigns value as an overt act ("coming to value that which is not valued"; see above). She even explicitly writes that: "Where we find happiness teaches us what we value rather than simply what is of value." (2010, 13). I suggest that this is the second decisive difference between a politically constructive, progressive normative style and a hegemonic one, beside their respective egalitarian vs. unegalitarian character: an alternative normative style is one that is explicit about assigning value – and thus, in establishing hierarchies of (political) priority – rather than naturalizing its own normative commitments. For instance, in critiquing inequality or normalizing, exclusionary features of dominant notions of happiness, Ahmed's writing explicitly commits itself to equality as a political value. I agree with her when, in referring to a contrary normative style that would reify hierarchies of value as intrinsically given (i.e. as inhering in subjects or objects themselves), Ahmed in the above example qualifies this as "a moral distinction [in which, C.B.] some forms of happiness are read as worth more than other forms of happiness". Schotten has similarly constructed queer theory in terms of (Nietzschean) "anti-morality" (2019, 213), critiquing morality as foreclosing critical contest, and as therefore depoliticizing (drawing on earlier interventions by Gayle Rubin and

Judith Butler) (Schotten 2019, 222–223). In line with the contrast drawn by Schotten between morality and politics, Schotten's and Ahmed's own discourses could, in contrast, be referred to as politicizing rather than moral, in that processes of naturalization or reification are here explicitly traced as such in a critical (egalitarian and anti-normalizing) spirit. Such denaturalization makes visible how power is entailed in discursive and other social processes that ostensibly are not about power; i.e. in which power is reified as a matter of 'nature' or 'fact' (cf. Schotten 2019, 222–223). I suggest that the latter forms the essence of a *normalizing* normative style: To declare something as 'normal' or 'abnormal' ('perverse'; 'pathological') is to *naturalize normativity*, and is thus to naturalize the very hierarchical relationship between these two terms that their distinction serves to establish (see chapter 4). It is to designate one's referent as *intrinsically* normal or abnormal, and thereby to render invisible the act or technology of normali*zation*. That is what both Schotten and Ahmed refer to in terms of the moral, and to which I would juxtapose the term "politicizing", understood as a practice oriented to rendering power relations and effects explicit. These practices – a normalizing, hegemonic style vs. a counter-hegemonic, egalitarian, denaturalizing normative style – could be qualified with a view to their relationship to power as power-evasive vs. power-cognizant, respectively, leaning on Ruth Frankenberg's terminology (1993). While a hegemonic normative style isn't *necessarily* normalizing, it can be identified by its anti-egalitarian and reifying character. (There might be other variants of such reification, after all, than a [specifically modern] [Foucault 1990, esp. 143–144] normalizing discourse.)

So, what I refer to as a politicizing, power-cognizant normative style is very much what Schotten qualifies as a (queer) discourse of "anti-morality". The problem with the latter designation is that it can be read as obfuscating the normative character of such discourse and that – contra Schotten – this is precisely to risk naturalizing the political effects, the power-effects, of (queer) discourse. In perpetuating the myth of a discourse innocent of power effects, distinguishing only between "morality" and "anti-morality", or the normative and anti- or nonnormative, is ultimately as un-Foucauldian as it is un-

Nietzschean (however Foucault and Nietzsche may themselves have understood their own respective discourses). For, the point that gets lost in such nomenclature is that moral *and* politicizing discourses are *both* normative, albeit in contrasting ways. To presume one's own discourse to be free of normativity or a 'will to power' would be profoundly uncritical.

Competing normative styles in Ahmed's discourse on happiness

Specified to the matter of happiness and unhappiness, an important task for an alternative, queer normative style is to denaturalize the ways in which "[h]appiness is expected to reside in certain places, those that approximate the taken-for-granted features of *normality*" (Ahmed 2007, 9; emphasis added). Such denaturalization would promote the recognition that there is no such thing as 'happiness as such'; that happiness only ever comes in alternative discursive framings, and that no one framing must be mistaken for 'happiness as such' (beyond its generic understanding as 'being affected positively', whatever that might mean to any one subject). For, it is a *naturalizing, reified* account of happiness that obscures the politically loaded character of hegemonic framings of the term, as critiqued by Ahmed (see above). For instance, constructions of happiness that Ahmed characterizes as coercive (2010, 91, 212) or disciplinary (2010, 8) in that they are aimed at compelling subjects to pursue very specific goals as a means to attaining happiness (so as to make others happy) can assume such a function only in virtue of naturalizing the connection between happiness and certain particular, supposed "happy objects". Denaturalization makes coercive prescriptions as to what happiness must mean to anyone the subject of critique, namely, for reifying a specific framing of 'happiness' which is then imposed upon others in the name of social conformity. Denaturalization thus makes discourses of happiness explicit as discourses and, as such, debatable. This forestalls their moral, coercively prescriptive character.

I venture the argument that 'happiness' construed in an alternative, normative but counter-hegemonic manner, as indicated above, is *not* subject to the critique Ahmed levels at conventional narratives of the term. Thus, in many strands of her argument in *The Promise of Happiness*, it is clear that the alternative framing of 'happiness' which she does offer (while at other times protesting that she does not want to offer such; see above) is non-dualistic in the sense that she refrains from playing off 'happiness' and 'unhappiness' against each other. This contrasts both with hegemonic notions of happiness and with affirmative feminism, as critiqued by Ahmed in Braidotti (see above). As we have seen earlier, sadness and other negative feelings in both of these discourses tend to be rejected – which rejection Ahmed argues results in socially excluding those associated with, or affected by, such feelings.

I see a clear instance of a counter-hegemonic, non-normalizing normative style in what earlier I have characterized as an egalitarian critique, advanced by Ahmed, of the unequal social distribution of happiness. It is neither 'for' nor 'against' unhappiness in any simple sense (unlike other strands of argument in *Promise*), but avows unhappiness as experienced by the unadjusted and subordinated as both a sad or negative state that some have to endure, and a state to be acknowledged – especially given that the hegemonic discourse of happiness, as sketched earlier, *contributes* to the unhappiness of those who will not or cannot conform. Due to the "happiness duty", or "compulsory happiness" (Stephens 2015, 277; see above), some pursue their own happiness at the cost of others (by urging social conformity upon them). This diagnosis exposes that it is unjust to reject or – put with a nod to psychoanalysis – to repudiate unhappiness or even suffering; to set up happiness and unhappiness as mutually exclusive opposites, one construed as positive and desirable, the other as abject. Ahmed in this strand of her argument in *Promise* is thus critiquing, on my reading, an approach to un-/happiness that operates on the model of a *reified hierarchical opposition*. Thus, she writes:

"I submit that if unhappiness cannot be willed away by the desire for happiness, then the desire for happiness can conceal signs of unhappiness or project them onto others who become symptoms of the failure to be happy. To desire only happiness in a world that involves tragedy is to ask others to bear the burden of that tragedy." (2010, 279, n. 12)

"The freedom to be unhappy is not about being wretched or sad, although it might involve freedom to express such feelings. The freedom to be unhappy would be the *freedom to be affected by what is unhappy*, and to live a life that might affect others unhappily." (2010, 195; emphasis added)

"It is thus possible to give an account of being happily queer that does not conceal signs of struggle." (2010, 118)

The relationship between happiness and unhappiness is here formulated as one of potential contiguity rather than of mutual exclusivity or repulsion, in which only one of these feelings would be avowed at the cost of the other. The openness or receptivity entailed in Ahmed's alternative formulations forestalls an exclusionary effect vis-à-vis those living with (the most) unhappiness. This is what enables the egalitarian trajectory of Ahmed's alternative framing of happiness, contrary to the ultimately unegalitarian (exclusionary) trajectory of the dualistic accounts offered by Braidotti – as read by Ahmed – as well as hegemonically.

But at other points in *The Promise of Happiness*, where Ahmed dismisses the association of happiness with what is good as intrinsically operating within the moral economy of happiness, she postulates an equally reified, inverted hierarchical opposition, as already indicated. This 'anti-happiness' strand of her argument, as it might be called, produces an exclusionary effect of its own – which I find coercive vis-à-vis those who avow happiness as good (as affecting subjects positively), in that to do so is dismissed as succumbing to hegemonic logic. As such, this move is unegalitarian, promoting affective social inequality even if it privileges unhappiness over happiness rather than the other way round. It also naturalizes, rather than denaturalizing, the normative hierarchy which Ahmed is establishing at this point in her account of happiness. Avowing happiness as good is here, after all, constructed as an orientation *intrinsically* subject to what she analyzes as the moral economy of happiness, thus ruling out in principle any counter-hegemonic point of view alternative to her own: Ahmed's own view is naturalized as intrinsically superior and enlightened, whereas any other perspective is a hegemonic perspective. (If elsewhere in *Promise*, Ahmed writes that "[h]appiness can involve an immanence of coercion, the demand for agreement" [2010, 212], I perceive the said move by her as demanding just such agreement in a rather coercive manner.) This is itself to mimic a hegemonic normative style, as characterized above. It is also clearly to contradict Ahmed's own avowals of an alternative framing of happiness, made elsewhere in the book (see above).

Conclusion: 'Counter-hegemonic/hegemonic' as a non-dualistic distinction

Only a non-dualistic framing of happiness and unhappiness, which refuses to dismiss *either* of these emotions, is truly egalitarian. In fact, Ahmed's critique of exclusionary framings of happiness – to the effect that these result in *social* exclusion and a devaluation of the unhappy (2010, 9) – is unintelligible in its critical force *except* when happiness is avowed as desirable (in virtue of affecting subjects positively). Otherwise, there could be nothing objectionable about the unequal social distribution of un-/happiness, and nothing desirable about seeing these affects distributed more equally amongst subjects. We can *both* avow as desirable the experience of 'being affected positively' (whether we refer to it as happiness, as joy or otherwise) *and simultaneously* acknowledge unhappiness as real, something that won't go away and without which political critique, resistance and struggle would be unthinkable – yet without 'hyping' pain and suffering, and without idealizing lives experienced as unlivable by those concerned. This would be to practice a politics that is self-consciously normative, *otherwise*: Namely, egalitarian and denaturalizing, rather than generating reified social hierarchies.

To be sure, the normative style framing Ahmed's egalitarian critique of hegemonic 'happiness' along these lines (as instantiated in parts of her argument, though not throughout *Promise*) is hierarchizing, too – *in a certain sense*. It is hierarchizing in the sense that critiquing an unequal social distribution of unhappiness is to imply that it would be just for happiness to be (more) equally distributed, and thus, that it is *better to feel happy than to feel bad or unhappy*. Happiness here, too, is thus being normatively privileged over and against unhappiness. Moreover, as we have seen, in "The Happiness Turn", Ahmed (2007) implicitly, but transparently privileges the take on happiness which she proposes (qua Cultural Studies' take) as better than the established approaches which she is questioning. This, too, is to establish a hierarchy of 'better' and 'worse' that is clearly normative. But this occurs in an *egalitarian* vein which contests affective *social* hierarchies (see above) that systematically privilege some categories of subjects over others, when it comes to access to happiness or – put in other terms – to being affected positively. Moreover, a counter-hegemonic normative style as I have characterized it in this chapter, based on Ahmed's writing about happiness, is overt about postulating a value hierarchy or a set of political priorities – thus acknowledging the potential for alternative priorities and, hence, the possibility of contesting any one set of values – rather than reifying any one such set as inhering in the objects which, or in the subjects who, are being constructed in its terms as their *intrinsic* value.

'Normativity' and 'antinormativity' have, alternatively, been construed in terms of a binary opposition, i.e. as mutually exclusive (as Wiegman and Wilson [2015] argue occurs in queer theory; an argument I find convincing) *or* the very difference between the two has been leveled (as happens when Wiegman and Wilson assert that there is no escaping a *normalizing* normativity [2015; see above and note 2 to this chapter; see also Wiegman 2012, Ch. 6]). These theoretical alternatives, taken together, resonate with the pattern of a meta-dualism of the kind identified by Lena Gunnarsson (2017) to pertain to separateness vs. inseparability or – as I have reread Gunnarsson in the Introduction to this book – between identity or affinity vs. (hypostatized) difference, one of which tends to be privileged one-sidedly at the cost of the other within the different context of feminist debates on intersectionality. In the queer-theoretical context to which I am referring here, both alternatives collude in a shared consensus that treats normativity and normalization as coextensive. It is this consensus that I wish to question, and to which I have sought to formulate a theoretical alternative through distinguishing between qualitatively (politically) different, hegemonic vs. counter-hegemonic normative styles. This alternative moves beyond the above meta-dualism that would have us either dilute the very distinction between queer antinormativity and a normalizing normativity, or would construct the former as an 'outside' to normativity altogether; as politically 'pure' or innocent.

As should be clear from this book as a whole, I propose the distinction between a hegemonic and a counter-hegemonic normative style – and conceive of the distinction between the terms 'hegemonic'/'counter-hegemonic', more generally – as a *non-dualistic distinction* (see chapter 1 for more on this notion). If counter-hegemonic and hegemonic moments of discourse conflict – which should be obvious and which we must surely hope they do – I would at the same time view their relationship as one of interdependency in the sense that they are mutually constitutive: On the one hand, as argued in chapter 3, the human subject is discursively constituted and, hence, resistance takes place in terms that cannot but relate in some way to discourses that have achieved a certain amount of hegemony. On the other hand, as chapter 3 has made equally apparent, it is at least partially in virtue of resistance (especially its affective dimension) that discourses transform over time, historically speaking. The relationship between hegemonic and counter-hegemonic discourses (as well as the practices framed in terms of them) can thus be viewed as chiastic: they are mutually implicated, yet distinct and even mutually antagonistic at the same time. In both of these aspects we are dealing with a relational distinction; in the strong sense that neither term is autonomous and in the weaker, yet equally important sense that the tension between hegemonic and counter-hegemonic practices *qualifies* as a form of relation or connection. This conception guards against the danger of a binary opposition that would situate the counter-hegemonic entirely outside of what it opposes, idealizing it as immune to political complicity and what Paul Gilroy has so felicitously described as "antagonistic indebtedness" (1993, 191).

The subject of this book – the persistence of dualism in much critical theory – attests to the power hegemonic discourses hold over even the most sustained efforts to move beyond them. I hope that this book has contributed in some small measure to this movement and, more specifically, to the collective undertaking of rendering poststructuralist theory as well as Cultural Studies *more* critical. 'Producing critical theory' is, in this sense, an unending task, rather than a goal that could be achieved in any final sense. In this chapter, I hope to have sketched constructively (based on Ahmed's example) what kind of progressive, even queer normative style might orient us in the labor of 'radicalizing' theory – as much as practice – further; of pushing ever further *beyond* any inadvertent complicities with unegalitarian discursive and social arrangements, including a normalizing, hegemonic normativity.

Bibliography

Ahmed, Sara (2006) *Queer Phenomenology: Orientations, Objects, Others.* Durham: Duke University Press.

Ahmed, Sara (2007) 'Editorial: The Happiness Turn.' *New Formations*, 63, Happiness, 7–14.

Ahmed, Sara (2008) 'Open Forum Imaginary Prohibitions: Some Preliminary Remarks on the Founding Gestures of the "New Materialism".' *European Journal of Women's Studies*, 15(1), 23–39.

Ahmed, Sara (2010) *The Promise of Happiness.* Durham: Duke University Press.

Ahmed, Sara (2014) *The Cultural Politics of Emotion.* Second edition. Edinburgh: Edinburgh University Press.

Alaimo, Stacy and Susan Hekman (2008) 'Introduction: Emerging Models of Materiality in Feminist Theory.' In: Stacy Alaimo and Susan Hekman (eds) *Material Feminisms.* Bloomington: Indiana University Press, pp. 1–19.

Amir, Merav and Hagar Kotef (2018) 'In-Secure Identities: On the Securitization of Abnormality.' *Environment and Planning D: Society and Space*, 36(2), 236–254.

Barad, Karen (2003) 'Posthumanist Performativity: Toward an Understanding of How Matter Comes to Matter.' *Signs*, 28(3), 801–831.

Barad, Karen (2007) *Meeting the Universe Halfway: Quantum Physics and the Entanglement of Matter and Meaning.* Durham: Duke University Press.

Bargetz, Brigitte (2015) 'The Distribution of Emotions: Affective Politics of Emancipation.' *Hypatia*, 30(3), 580–596.

Bargetz, Brigitte and Gundula Ludwig (2015) 'Bausteine einer queerfeministischen politischen Theorie: Eine Einleitung.' *Femina Politica*, 1, 9–24.

Barnett, Clive (2008) 'Political Affects in Public Space: Normative Blind-Spots in Non-Representational Ontologies.' *Transactions of the Institute of British Geographers*, 33(2), 186–200.

Barnwell, Ashley (2016) 'Creative Paranoia: Affect and Social Method.' *Emotion, Space and Society*, 20, 10–17.

Barthes, Roland (2006a) 'Myth Today.' In: John Storey (ed) *Cultural Theory and Popular Culture: A Reader*. Third edition. Prentice Hall: Pearson, pp. 261–269.

Barthes, Roland (2006b) 'The Reality Effect.' In: Dorothy J. Hale (ed) *The Novel: An Anthology of Criticism and Theory, 1900–2000*. Malden etc.: Blackwell, pp. 229–234.

Benjamin, Jessica (1988) *The Bonds of Love: Psychoanalysis, Feminism, and the Problem of Domination*. New York: Pantheon Books.

Bennett, Jane (2010) *Vibrant Matter: A Political Ecology of Things*. Durham and London: Duke University Press.

Berlant, Lauren (ed) (2004) *Compassion: The Culture and Politics of an Emotion*. New York and London: Routledge.

Berlant, Lauren and Michael Warner (1998) 'Sex in Public.' *Critical Inquiry*, 24(2), Intimacy, 547–566.

Bhabha, Homi K. (1994) *The Location of Culture*. Abingdon and New York: Routledge.

Birla, Ritu (2010) 'Postcolonial Studies: Now That's History.' In Rosalind C. Morris (ed) *Can the Subaltern Speak? Reflections on the History of an Idea*. New York: Columbia University Press, pp. 87–99.

Bordo, Susan (1986) 'The Cartesian Masculinization of Thought.' *Signs*, 11(3), 439–456.

Braidotti, Rosi (2002) *Metamorphoses: Towards a Materialist Theory of Becoming*. Cambridge: Polity.

Braunmühl, Caroline (2012a) *Colonial Discourse and Gender in U.S. Criminal Courts: Cultural Defenses and Prosecutions*. New York: Routledge.

Braunmühl, Caroline (2012b) 'Theorizing Emotions with Judith Butler: Within and Beyond the Courtroom.' *Rethinking History*, 16(2), 221–240.

Bruining, Dennis (2013) 'A Somatechnics of Moralism: New Materialism or Material Foundationalism.' *Somatechnics*, 3(1), 149–168.

Bruining, Dennis (2016) 'Interrogating the Founding Gestures of the New Materialism.' *Cultural Studies Review*, 22(2), 21–40. https://dx.doi.org/10.5130/csr.v22i2.4461

Butler, Judith (1990) *Gender Trouble: Feminism and the Subversion of Identity*. New York and London: Routledge.

Butler, Judith (1992) 'Contingent Foundations: Feminism and the Question of "Postmodernism".' In: Judith Butler and Joan W. Scott (eds) *Feminists Theorize the Political*. New York: Routledge, pp. 3–21.

Butler, Judith (1993) *Bodies That Matter: On the Discursive Limits of "Sex"*. New York and London: Routledge.

Butler, Judith (1997) *The Psychic Life of Power: Theories in Subjection*. Stanford: Stanford University Press.

Butler, Judith (2003) *Kritik der ethischen Gewalt: Adorno-Vorlesungen 2002*. Trans. Reiner Ansén. Frankfurt am Main: Suhrkamp Verlag.

Butler, Judith (2004a) *Precarious Life: The Powers of Mourning and Violence*. London and New York: Verso.

Butler, Judith (2004b) *Undoing Gender*. New York and London: Routledge.

Butler, Judith (2005) *Giving an Account of Oneself*. New York: Fordham University Press.

Butler, Judith (2009) *Krieg und Affekt*. Trans. Eva Redecker, Judith Mohrmann and Juliane Rebentisch. Zürich and Berlin: diaphanes.

Butler, Judith (2010) *Frames of War: When is Life Grievable?* London and New York: Verso.

Butler, Judith (2012a) 'Can One Lead a Good Life in a Bad Life? Adorno Prize Lecture.' *Radical Philosophy*, 176, 9–18.

Butler, Judith (2012b) *Subjects of Desire: Hegelian Reflections in Twentieth-Century France*. New York: Columbia University Press.

Butler, Judith (2015a) *Notes Toward a Performative Theory of Assembly*. Cambridge: Harvard University Press.

Butler, Judith (2015b) *Senses of the Subject*. New York: Fordham University Press.

Caserio, Robert L. *et al.* (2006) 'The Antisocial Thesis in Queer Theory.' *PMLA*, 121(3), 819–828.

Castel, Robert (1991) 'From Dangerousness to Risk.' In: Graham Burchell, Colin Gordon and Peter Miller (eds) *The Foucault Effect: Studies in Governmentality.* Chicago: Chicago University Press, pp. 281–298.

Chambers, Samuel A. (2017) 'On Norms and Opposition.' *No Foundations: An Interdisciplinary Journal of Law and Justice*, 14, 1–26.

Coleman, Rebecca (2014) 'Inventive Feminist Theory: Representation, Materiality and Intensive Time.' *Women: A Cultural Review*, 25(1), 27–45.

Coole, Diana (2000) *Negativity and Politics: Dionysos and Dialectics from Kant to Poststructuralism.* London and New York: Routledge.

Coole, Diana and Samantha Frost (2010) 'Introducing the New Materialisms.' In: Diana Coole and Samantha Frost (eds) *New Materialisms: Ontology, Agency, and Politics.* Durham and London: Duke University Press, pp. 1–43.

Crenshaw, Kimberlé (1991) 'Mapping the Margins: Intersectionality, Identity Politics, and Violence Against Women of Color.' *Stanford Law Review*, 43(6), 1241–1299.

Cromby, John and Martin E. H. Willis (2016) 'Affect – Or Feeling (After Leys).' *Theory and Psychology*, 26(4), 476–495.

Cvetkovich, Ann (2012) *Depression: A Public Feeling.* Durham: Duke University Press.

Davis, Noela (2009) 'New Materialism and Feminism's Anti-Biologism: A Response to Sara Ahmed.' *European Journal of Women's Studies*, 16(1), 67–80.

Davis, Noela (2014) 'Politics Materialized: Rethinking the Materiality of Feminist Political Action through Epigenetics.' *Women: A Cultural Review*, 25(1), 62–77.

Deleuze, Gilles and Michel Foucault (1980) 'Intellectuals and Power: A Conversation Between Michel Foucault and Gilles Deleuze.' In: Michel Foucault, *Language, Counter-Memory, Practice: Selected Essays and Interviews*. Ed. Donald F. Bouchard. Trans. Donald F. Bouchard and Sherry Simon. Ithaca: Cornell University Press, 205–217.

Derrida, Jacques (1976) *Of Grammatology*. Trans. Gayatri C. Spivak. Baltimore: John Hopkins University Press.

Duggan, Lisa (2004) *The Twilight of Equality? Neoliberalism, Cultural Politics, and the Attack on Democracy*. Boston: Beacon Press.

Edelman, Lee (2004) *No Future: Queer Theory and the Death Drive*. Durham: Duke University Press.

Elden, Stuart (2007) 'Governmentality, Calculation, Territory.' *Environment and Planning D: Society and Space*, 25(3), 562–580.

Engel, Antke (2002) *Wider die Eindeutigkeit: Sexualität und Geschlecht im Fokus queerer Politik der Repräsentation*. Frankfurt am Main and New York: Campus.

Engel, Antke (2009) *Bilder von Sexualität und Ökonomie: Queere kulturelle Politiken im Neoliberalismus*. Bielefeld: transcript.

Fairclough, Norman (1989) *Language and Power*. London: Longman.

Fanon, Frantz (1986) *Black Skin, White Masks*. Trans. Charles L. Markman. London: Pluto Press.

Ferguson, Kathy E. (1993) *The Man Question: Visions of Subjectivity in Feminist Theory*. Berkeley: University of California Press.

Ferguson, Roderick A. (2004) *Aberrations in Black: Toward a Queer of Color Critique*. Minneapolis: University of Minnesota Press.

Fischer, Clara (2016) 'Feminist Philosophy, Pragmatism, and the "Turn to Affect": A Genealogical Critique.' *Hypatia*, 31(4), 810–826.

Flax, Jane (1993) *Disputed Subjects: Essays on Psychoanalysis, Politics and Philosophy*. New York and London: Routledge.

Foucault, Michel (1972) *The Archeology of Knowledge*. Trans. A. M. Sheridan Smith. London: Routledge.

Foucault, Michel (1980) 'Truth and Power.' In: Michel Foucault, *Power/Knowledge: Selected Interviews and Other Writings, 1972–1977*. Ed. Colin Gordon. Trans. Colin Gordon *et al*. New York: Pantheon Books, pp. 109–133.

Foucault, Michel (1982) 'Afterword: The Subject and Power.' In: Hubert L. Dreyfus and Paul Rabinow, *Michel Foucault: Beyond Structuralism and Hermeneutics*. New York etc.: Harvester Wheatsheaf, pp. 208–226.

Foucault, Michel (1984) 'What is Enlightenment?' In: Paul Rabinow (ed) *The Foucault Reader*. New York: Pantheon Books, pp. 32–50.

Foucault, Michel (1990) *The History of Sexuality, Volume 1: An Introduction*. Trans. Robert Hurley. London etc.: Penguin Books.

Foucault, Michel (1991) *Discipline and Punish: The Birth of the Prison*. Trans. Alan Sheridan. London etc.: Penguin Books.

Foucault, Michel (1994) 'L'extension sociale de la norme.' In: Michel Foucault, *Dits et écrits 1954–1988*. Vol. III 1976–1979. Ed. Daniel Defert and François Ewald under the collaboration of Jacques Lagrange. Paris: Éditions Gallimard, pp. 74–79.

Foucault, Michel (1999) *Les Anormaux: Cours au Collège de France, 1974–75*. Ed. Valerio Marchetti and Antonella Salomoni. General eds: François Ewald and Alessandro Fontana. Paris: Éditions de Seuil/ Gallimard.

Foucault, Michel (2003) *Abnormal: Lectures at the Collège de France, 1974–1975*. Ed. Valerio Marchetti and Antonella Salomoni. General eds: François Ewald and Alessandro Fontana. English Series Ed: Arnold I. Davidson. Trans. Graham Burchell. New York: Picador.

Foucault, Michel (2004) *"Society Must Be Defended": Lectures at the Collège de France, 1975–1976*. Ed. Mauro Bertani and Alessandro Fontana. General eds: François Ewald and Alessandro Fontana. English Series Ed: Arnold I. Davidson. Trans. David Macey. London etc.: Penguin Books.

Foucault, Michel (2007) *Security, Territory, Population: Lectures at the Collège de France, 1977–78*. Ed. Michel Senellart. General eds: François Ewald and Alessandro Fontana. English Series Ed: Arnold I. Davidson. Trans. Graham Burchell. New York: Palgrave Macmillan.

Foucault, Michel (2010) *The Birth of Biopolitics: Lectures at the Collège de France, 1978–1979*. Ed. Michel Senellart. General eds: François Ewald and Alessandro Fontana. English Series Ed: Arnold I. Davidson. Trans. Graham Burchell. New York: Palgrave Macmillan.

Frankenberg, Ruth (1993) *White Women, Race Matters: The Social Construction of Whiteness*. Minneapolis: University of Minnesota Press.

Fraser, Nancy (2013) *Fortunes of Feminism: From State-Managed Capitalism to Neoliberal Crisis.* London and New York: Verso.

Freud, Sigmund (1989) *Civilization and Its Discontents.* Trans. and ed. James Strachey. New York: Norton.

Frost, Samantha (2014) 'Re-Considering the Turn to Biology in Feminist Theory.' *Feminist Theory*, 15(3), 307–326.

Gilroy, Paul (1987) *There Ain't No Black in the Union Jack: The Cultural Politics of Race and Nation.* London: Hutchinson.

Gilroy, Paul (1993) *The Black Atlantic: Modernity and Double Consciousness.* London and New York: Verso.

Gramsci, Antonio (1971) *Selections from the Prison Notebooks of Antonio Gramsci.* Ed. and trans. Quintin Hoare and Geoffrey N. Smith. London: Lawrence & Wishart.

Gunnarsson, Lena (2013) 'The Naturalistic Turn in Feminist Theory: A Marxist-Realist Contribution.' *Feminist Theory*, 14(1), 3–19.

Gunnarsson, Lena (2017) 'Why We Keep Separating the "Inseparable": Dialecticizing Intersectionality.' *European Journal of Women's Studies*, 24(2), 114–127.

Gutiérrez Rodríguez, Encarnación (2007) '"Sexuelle Multitude" und prekäre Subjektivitäten: Queers, Prekarisierung und transnationaler Feminismus.' In: Marianne Pieper *et al.* (eds) *Empire und die biopolitische Wende: Die internationale Diskussion im Anschluss an Hardt und Negri.* Frankfurt am Main: Campus, pp. 125–139.

Halberstam, Judith (Jack) (2011) *The Queer Art of Failure.* Durham: Duke University Press.

Hall, Donald E. and Annamarie Jagose (2013) 'Introduction: The Queer Turn.' In: Donald E. Hall and Annamarie Jagose, with Andrea Bebell and Susan Potter (eds) *The Routledge Queer Studies Reader.* New York: Routledge, pp. xiv–xx.

Hall, Radclyffe (1982) *The Well of Loneliness.* London: Virago Press.

Hall, Stuart (1996) 'New Ethnicities.' In: David Morley and Kuan-Hsing Chen (eds) *Stuart Hall: Critical Dialogues in Cultural Studies.* London and New York: Routledge, pp. 442–451.

Happy-Go-Lucky (2008) Dir. Mike Leigh. Momentum Pictures.

Haraway, Donna J. (1991) 'Situated Knowledges: The Science Question in Feminism and the Privilege of Partial Perspective.' In: Donna J. Haraway, *Simians, Cyborgs, and Women: The Reinvention of Nature*. New York: Routledge, pp. 183–201.

Haraway, Donna J. (2008) *When Species Meet*. Minneapolis and London: University of Minnesota Press.

Hardt, Michael and Antonio Negri (2001) *Empire*. Cambridge and London: Harvard University Press.

Hardt, Michael and Antonio Negri (2004) *Multitude: War and Democracy in the Age of Empire*. New York: Penguin Press.

Haritaworn, Jin (2015) *Queer Lovers and Hateful Others: Regenerating Violent Times and Places*. London: Pluto Press.

Hark, Sabine (1999) 'deviante Subjekte [sic]: Normalisierung und Subjektformierung.' In: Werner Sohn and Herbert Mehrtens (eds) *Normalität und Abweichung: Studien zur Theorie und Geschichte der Normalisierungsgesellschaft*. Opladen and Wiesbaden: Westdeutscher Verlag, pp. 65–84.

Hark, Sabine (2000) 'Durchquerung des Rechts: Paradoxien einer Politik der Rechte.' In: quaestio (ed) *Queering Demokratie: Sexuelle Politiken*. Berlin: Querverlag, pp. 28–44.

Haroche, Claudine, Paul Henry and Michel Pêcheux (1971) 'La Sémantique et la Coupure Saussurienne: Langue, Langage, Discours.' *Langages*, 24, 93–106.

Hemmings, Clare (2005) 'Invoking Affect: Cultural Theory and the Ontological Turn.' *Cultural Studies*, 19(5), 548–567.

Hemmings, Clare (2011) *Why Stories Matter: The Political Grammar of Feminist Theory*. Durham and London: Duke University Press.

Hinton, Peta (2013) 'The Quantum Dance and the World's "Extraordinary Liveliness": Refiguring Corporeal Ethics in Karen Barad's Agential Realism.' *Somatechnics*, 3(1), 169–189.

Hinton, Peta and Xin Liu (2015) 'The Im/Possibility of Abandonment in New Materialist Ontologies.' *Australian Feminist Studies*, 30(84), 128–145.

Hird, Myra J. (2004) 'Feminist Matters: New Materialist Considerations of Sexual Difference.' *Feminist Theory*, 5(2), 223–232.

Hird, Myra J. and Celia Roberts (2011) 'Feminism Theorises the Nonhuman.' *Feminist Theory*, 12(2), 109–117.

Hochschild, Arlie Russell (2003) *The Managed Heart: Commercialization of Human Feeling*. Twentieth anniversary edition with a new afterword. Berkeley: University of California Press.

hooks, bell (2006) 'Eating the Other: Desire and Resistance.' In: Meenakshi Gigi Durham and Douglas M. Kellner (eds) *Media and Cultural Studies: KeyWorks*. Revised edition. Malden etc.: Blackwell, pp. 366–380.

Hull, Akasha (Gloria T.), Patricia Bell-Scott and Barbara Smith (eds) (2015) *All the Women Are White, All the Blacks Are Men, But Some of Us Are Brave: Black Women's Studies*. Second edition. With a new afterword by Brittney Cooper. New York: The Feminist Press at the City University of New York.

Hulme, Peter and Ludmilla Jordanova (eds) (1990) *The Enlightenment and Its Shadows*. London: Routledge.

Hutta, Jan S. (2015) 'The Affective Life of Semiotics.' *Geographica Helvetica*, 70, 295–309.

Illouz, Eva (2008) *Saving the Modern Soul: Therapy, Emotions, and the Culture of Self-Help*. Berkeley: University of California Press.

Irni, Sari (2013) 'The Politics of Materiality: Affective Encounters in a Transdisciplinary Debate.' *European Journal of Women's Studies*, 20(4), 347–360.

Jagger, Gill (2015) 'The New Materialism and Sexual Difference.' *Signs*, 40(2), 321–342.

Jagose, Annamarie (2015) 'The Trouble with Antinormativity.' *differences*, 26(1), Antinormativity's queer conventions, 26–47.

Kelly, Mark (2019) 'What's in a Norm? Foucault's Conceptualization and Genealogy of the Norm.' *Foucault Studies*, 27, 1–22. https://doi.org/1 0.22439/fs.v27i27.5889

Kirby, Vicki (2011) *Quantum Anthropologies: Life at Large*. Durham and London: Duke University Press.

Koivunen, Anu (2010) 'An Affective Turn? Reimagining the Subject of Feminist Theory.' In: Marianne Liljeström and Susanna Paasonen (eds) *Working with Affects in Feminist Readings: Disturbing Differences.* New York: Routledge, pp. 8–28.

Laclau, Ernesto (1990) 'New Reflections on the Revolution of Our Time.' In: Ernesto Laclau, *New Reflections on the Revolution of Our Time.* London and New York: Verso, pp. 3–85.

Le Guin, Ursula K. (1987) 'The Ones Who Walk Away from Omelas.' In: Ursula K. Le Guin, *The Wind's Twelve Quarters.* New York: Perennial.

Lemke, Thomas (2007) *Gouvernementalität und Biopolitik.* Wiesbaden: VS Verlag für Sozialwissenschaften.

Leys, Ruth (2011) 'The Turn to Affect: A Critique.' *Critical Inquiry*, 37, 434–472.

Leys, Ruth (2017) *The Ascent of Affect: Genealogy and Critique.* Chicago: The University of Chicago Press.

Link, Jürgen (1998) 'Von der "Macht der Norm" zum "flexiblen Normalismus": Überlegungen nach Foucault.' In Joseph Jurt (ed) *Zeitgenössische französische Denker: Eine Bilanz.* Freiburg: Rombach Verlag, pp. 251–268.

Link, Jürgen (2004) 'From the "Power of the Norm" to "Flexible Normalism": Considerations after Foucault.' Trans. Mirko M. Hall. *Cultural Critique*, 57, 14–32.

Link, Jürgen (2013) *Normale Krisen? Normalismus und die Krise der Gegenwart.* Konstanz: Konstanz University Press.

Lorde, Audre (1984) *Sister Outsider: Essays and Speeches.* Trumansburg: Crossing Press.

Lorey, Isabell (2011) *Figuren des Immunen: Elemente einer politischen Theorie.* Zürich: diaphanes.

Lorey, Isabell (2015) *State of Insecurity: Government of the Precarious.* With a foreword by Judith Butler. Trans. Aileen Derieg. London and New York: Verso.

Lorey, Isabell, Gundula Ludwig and Ruth Sonderegger (2016) 'Foucaults Gegenwart. Sexualität – Sorge – Revolution.' In: Isabell Lorey, Gundula Ludwig and Ruth Sonderegger, *Foucaults Gegenwart: Sexualität – Sorge – Revolution.* Wien: transversal texts, pp. 9–13.

Love, Heather (2007a) 'Compulsory Happiness and Queer Existence.' *New Formations*, 63, Happiness, 52–64.

Love, Heather (2007b) *Feeling Backward: Loss and the Politics of Queer History*. Cambridge: Harvard University Press.

Ludwig, Gundula (2016a) 'Desiring Neoliberalism.' *Sexuality Research and Social Policy*, 13, 417–427. https://doi.org/10.1007/s13178-016-0257-6

Ludwig, Gundula (2016b) 'Freiheitsversprechen und Technologien der Macht: Transformationen des Sexualitätsdispositivs und das Begehren nach dem neoliberalen Staat.' In: Isabell Lorey, Gundula Ludwig and Ruth Sonderegger, *Foucaults Gegenwart: Sexualität – Sorge – Revolution*. Wien: transversal texts, pp. 15–45.

Macdonnell, Diane (1986) *Theories of Discourse: An Introduction*. New York: Blackwell.

Mardorossian, Carine M. (2002) 'Toward a New Feminist Theory of Rape.' *Signs*, 27(3), 743–775.

Massumi, Brian (2002) *Parables for the Virtual: Movement, Affect, Sensation*. Durham: Duke University Press.

May, Todd (2005) *Gilles Deleuze: An Introduction*. Cambridge etc.: Cambridge University Press.

May, Todd and Ladelle McWhorter (2015) 'Who's Being Disciplined Now? Operations of Power in a Neoliberal World.' In: Vernon W. Cisney and Nicolae Morar (eds) *Biopower: Foucault and Beyond*. Chicago: Chicago University Press, pp. 245–258.

McAvoy, Jean (2015) 'From Ideology to Feeling: Discourse, Emotion, and an Analytic Synthesis.' *Qualitative Research in Psychology*, 12(1), 22–33.

McNeil, Maureen (2011) 'Post-Millennial Feminist Theory: Encounters with Humanism, Materialism, Critique, Nature, Biology and Darwin.' *Journal for Cultural Research*, 14(4), 427–437.

McWhorter, Ladelle (2012) 'Queer Economies.' *Foucault Studies*, 14, 61–78. https://doi.org/10.22439/fs.v0i14.3891

McWhorter, Ladelle (2017) 'From Scientific Racism to Neoliberal Biopolitics.' In: Naomi Zack (ed) *The Oxford Handbook of Philosophy and Race*. Oxford: Oxford University Press, pp. 282–293.

Mesquita, Sushila (2012) 'Recht und Heteronormativität im Wandel.' In: Helga Haberler *et al.* (eds) *Que[e]r zum Staat: Heteronormativitätskritische Perspektiven auf Staat, Macht, Gesellschaft*. Berlin: Querverlag, pp. 42–60.

Muñoz, José E. (2009) *Cruising Utopia: The Then and There of Queer Futurity.* New York: New York University Press.

Nussbaum, Martha C. (2001) *Upheavals of Thought: The Intelligence of Emotions.* Cambridge: Cambridge University Press.

Patton, Paul (2000) *Deleuze and the Political.* London and New York: Routledge.

Pêcheux, Michel (1982) *Language, Semantics and Ideology: Stating the Obvious.* Trans. Harbans Nagpal. London: Macmillan Press.

Pedwell, Carolyn (2012a) 'Affective (Self-) Transformations: Empathy, Neoliberalism and International Development.' *Feminist Theory*, 13(2), 163–179.

Pedwell, Carolyn (2012b) 'Economies of Empathy: Obama, Neoliberalism, and Social Justice.' *Environment and Planning D: Society and Space*, 30(2), 280–297.

Pedwell, Carolyn (2013) 'Affect at the Margins: Alternative Empathies in *A Small Place*.' *Emotion, Space and Society*, 8, 18–26.

Pedwell, Carolyn (2014) 'Cultural Theory As Mood Work.' *New Formations*, 82, Mood work, 47–63.

Potter, Jonathan *et al.* (1990) 'Discourse: Noun, Verb or Social Practice?' *Philosophical Psychology*, 3(2), 205–217.

Puig de la Bellacasa, María (2010) 'Ethical Doings in Naturecultures.' *Ethics, Place and Environment*, 13(2), 151–169.

Reddy, William M. (2001) *The Navigation of Feeling: A Framework for the History of Emotions.* Cambridge: Cambridge University Press.

Reddy, William M. (2008) 'Against Constructionism: The Historical Ethnography of Emotions.' In: Monica Greco and Paul Stenner (eds) *Emotions: A Social Science Reader.* London: Routledge, pp. 72–83.

Rehmann, Jan (2016) 'The Unfulfilled Promises of the Late Foucault and Foucauldian "Governmentality Studies".' In: Daniel Zamora and Michael C. Behrent (eds) *Foucault and Neoliberalism.* Cambridge and Malden: Polity, pp. 134–158.

Richardson, Diane (2005) 'Desiring Sameness? The Rise of a Neoliberal Politics of Normalisation.' *Antipode*, 37(3), 515–535.

Sauer, Birgit *et al.* (2017) 'Exclusive Intersections: Constructions of Gender and Sexuality.' In: Gabriella Lazaridis and Giovanna

Campani (eds) *Understanding the Populist Shift: Othering in a Europe in Crisis*. London and New York: Routledge, pp. 104–121.

Schotten, C. Heike (2019) 'Nietzsche and Emancipatory Politics: Queer Theory as Anti-Morality.' *Critical Sociology*, 45(2), 213–226.

Sedgwick, Eve K. (2003) *Touching Feeling: Affect, Pedagogy, Performativity*. Durham: Duke University Press.

Snediker, Michael D. (2009) *Queer Optimism: Lyric Personhood and Other Felicitous Persuasions*. Minneapolis: University of Minnesota Press.

Spindler, Susanne (2006) *Corpus delicti: Männlichkeit, Rassismus und Kriminalisierung im Alltag jugendlicher Migranten*. Münster: Unrast Verlag.

Spinoza, Benedict de (2018) *Ethics: Proved in Geometrical Order*. Ed. Matthew J. Kisner. Trans. Michael Silverthorne and Matthew J. Kisner. Cambridge: Cambridge University Press.

Spivak, Gayatri C. (1985) 'The Rani of Sirmur: An Essay in Reading the Archives.' *History and Theory*, 24(3), 247–272.

Spivak, Gayatri C. (1988a) 'Can the Subaltern Speak?' In: Cary Nelson and Lawrence Grossberg (eds) *Marxism and the Interpretation of Culture*. Urbana: University of Illinois Press, pp. 271–313.

Spivak, Gayatri C. (1988b) 'French Feminism in an International Frame.' In: Gayatri C. Spivak, *In Other Worlds: Essays in Cultural Politics*. New York and London: Routledge, pp. 134–153.

Spivak, Gayatri C. (1988c) 'Subaltern Studies: Deconstructing Historiography.' In: Gayatri C. Spivak, *In Other Worlds: Essays in Cultural Politics*. New York and London: Routledge, pp. 197–221.

Spivak, Gayatri C. (1990) *The Post-Colonial Critic: Interviews, Strategies, Dialogues*. Ed. Sarah Harasym. New York and London: Routledge.

Spivak, Gayatri C. (1994) 'Bonding in Difference.' In: Alfred Arteaga (ed) *An Other Tongue: Nation and Ethnicity in the Linguistic Borderlands*. Durham: Duke University Press, pp. 273–285.

Spivak, Gayatri C. (2012) *An Aesthetic Education in the Era of Globalization*. Cambridge and London: Harvard University Press.

Stacey, Jackie (2014) 'Wishing Away Ambivalence.' *Feminist Theory*, 15(1), 39–49.

Stephens, Elizabeth (2015) 'Bad Feelings.' *Australian Feminist Studies*, 30(85), 273–282.

Stoler, Ann L. (2015) 'A Colonial Reading of Foucault: Bourgeois Bodies and Racial Selves.' In: Vernon W. Cisney and Nicolae Morar (eds) *Biopower: Foucault and Beyond*. Chicago: Chicago University Press, pp. 326–347.

Sullivan, Nikki (2012) 'The Somatechnics of Perception and the Matter of the Non/Human: A Critical Response to the New Materialism.' *European Journal of Women's Studies*, 19(3), 299–313.

Thesing, Peet (2017) *Feministische Psychiatriekritik*. Münster: Unrast Verlag.

Thrift, Nigel (2008) *Non-Representational Theory: Space, Politics, Affect*. London: Routledge.

Tuana, Nancy (2008) 'Viscous Porosity: Witnessing Katrina.' In: Stacy Alaimo and Susan Hekman (eds) *Material Feminisms*. Bloomington: Indiana University Press, pp. 188–213.

Tyler, Imogen (2013) *Revolting Subjects: Social Abjection and Resistance in Neoliberal Britain*. London and New York: Zed Books.

van der Tuin, Iris (2008) 'Deflationary Logic: Response to Sara Ahmed's "Imaginary Prohibitions: Some Preliminary Remarks on the Founding Gestures of the 'New Materialism'".' *European Journal of Women's Studies*, 15(4), 411–416.

Vaughan, Megan (1991) *Curing Their Ills: Colonial Power and African Illness*. Stanford: Stanford University Press.

Villa, Paula-Irene (2008) 'Habe den Mut, Dich Deines Körpers zu bedienen! Thesen zur Körperarbeit in der Gegenwart zwischen Selbstermächtigung und Selbstunterwerfung.' In: Paula-Irene Villa (ed) *schön normal* [sic]: *Manipulationen am Körper als Technologien des Selbst*. Bielefeld: transcript, pp. 245–272.

von Osten, Marion (2003) 'Einleitung.' In: Marion von Osten (ed) *Norm der Abweichung*. Wien etc.: Springer, pp. 7–18.

Weiner, Joshua J. and Damon Young (2011) 'Queer Bonds.' *GLQ: A Journal of Lesbian and Gay Studies*, 17(2–3), Queer bonds, 223–241.

Wetherell, Margaret (2012) *Affect and Emotion: A New Social Science Understanding*. Los Angeles: Sage.

Wetherell, Margaret (2015) 'Trends in the Turn to Affect: A Social Psychological Critique.' *Body and Society*, 1(2), 139–166.

Wetherell, Margaret and Jonathan Potter (1992) *Mapping the Language of Racism: Discourse and the Legitimation of Exploitation*. New York: Harvester Wheatsheaf.

Wiegman, Robyn (2012) *Object Lessons*. Durham: Duke University Press.

Wiegman, Robyn and Elizabeth A. Wilson (2015) 'Introduction: Antinormativity's Queer Conventions.' *differences*, 26(1), Antinormativity's queer conventions, 1–25.

Willey, Angela (2016) 'Biopossibility: A Queer Feminist Materialist Science Studies Manifesto, with Special Reference to the Question of Monogamous Behavior.' *Signs*, 41(3), 553–577.

Winnubst, Shannon (2012) 'The Queer Thing about Neoliberal Pleasure: A Foucauldian Warning.' *Foucault Studies*, 14, 79–97. https://doi.org/10.22439/fs.v0i14.3889

Zamora, Daniel and Michael C. Behrent (eds) (2016) *Foucault and Neoliberalism*. Cambridge and Malden: Polity.

Cultural Studies

Gabriele Klein
Pina Bausch's Dance Theater
Company, Artistic Practices and Reception

2020, 440 p., pb., col. ill.
29,99 € (DE), 978-3-8376-5055-6
E-Book:
PDF: 29,99 € (DE), ISBN 978-3-8394-5055-0

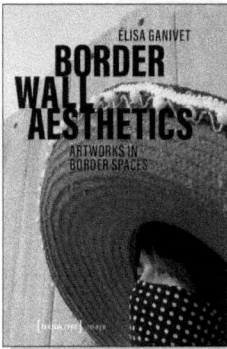

Elisa Ganivet
Border Wall Aesthetics
Artworks in Border Spaces

2019, 250 p., hardcover, ill.
79,99 € (DE), 978-3-8376-4777-8
E-Book:
PDF: 79,99 € (DE), ISBN 978-3-8394-4777-2

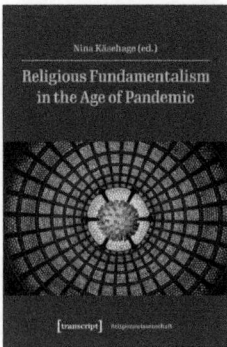

Nina Käsehage (ed.)
**Religious Fundamentalism
in the Age of Pandemic**

April 2021, 278 p., pb., col. ill.
37,00 € (DE), 978-3-8376-5485-1
E-Book: available as free open access publication
PDF: ISBN 978-3-8394-5485-5

**All print, e-book and open access versions of the titles in our list
are available in our online shop www.transcript-publishing.com**

Cultural Studies

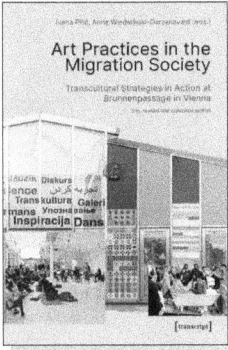

Ivana Pilic, Anne Wiederhold-Daryanavard (eds.)
Art Practices in the Migration Society
Transcultural Strategies in Action
at Brunnenpassage in Vienna

March 2021, 244 p., pb.
29,00 € (DE), 978-3-8376-5620-6
E-Book:
PDF: 25,99 € (DE), ISBN 978-3-8394-5620-0

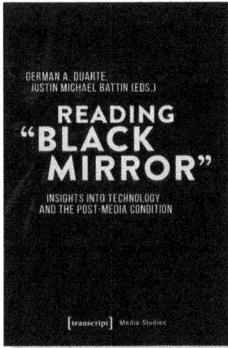

German A. Duarte, Justin Michael Battin (eds.)
Reading »Black Mirror«
Insights into Technology and the Post-Media Condition

January 2021, 334 p., pb.
32,00 € (DE), 978-3-8376-5232-1
E-Book:
PDF: 31,99 € (DE), ISBN 978-3-8394-5232-5

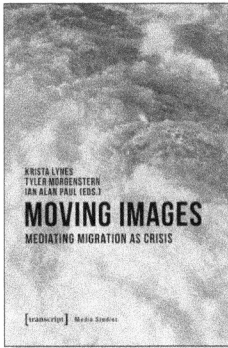

Krista Lynes, Tyler Morgenstern, Ian Alan Paul (eds.)
Moving Images
Mediating Migration as Crisis

2020, 320 p., pb., col. ill.
40,00 € (DE), 978-3-8376-4827-0
E-Book: available as free open access publication
PDF: ISBN 978-3-8394-4827-4

GPSR Authorized Representative: Easy Access System Europe, Mustamäe tee
50, 10621 Tallinn, Estonia, gpsr.requests@easproject.com